THE TWILIGHT HOURS

Teachings for HU-man Development from Saint Germain

ALSO BY LORI TOYE

The
Twilight
Hours

Teachings for HU-man Development
from Saint Germain

LORI ADAILE TOYE

I AM AMERICA PUBLISHING & DISTRIBUTING
P.O. Box 2511, Payson, Arizona, 85547, USA.
www.iamamerica.com

© (Copyright) 2020 by Lori Adaile Toye. All rights reserved.
ISBN: 978-1-880050-40-8

All rights exclusively reserved, including under the Berne Convention and the
Universal Copyright Convention. No part of this book may be reproduced or
translated into any language or utilized in any form or by any means, electronic
or mechanical, including photocopying, recording, or by any information storage
and retrieval system, without written permission from the publisher. Published
in 2020 by I AM America Seventh Ray Publishing International, P.O. Box 2511,
Payson, Arizona, 85547, United States of America.

I AM America Maps and Books have been marketed since 1989 by I AM America
Seventh Ray Publishing and Distributing, through workshops, conferences, and
numerous bookstores in the United States and internationally. If you are interested
in obtaining information on available releases please write:
I AM America, P.O. Box 2511, Payson, Arizona, 85547
or visit:

www.iamamerica.com
www.loritoye.com

Graphic Design and Typography by Lori Toye
Editing by Elaine Cardall

Love, in service, breathes the breath for all!

10 9 8 7 6 5 4 3 2 1

"HU-mans you shall be!"

~ SAINT GERMAIN

Contents

CHAPTER TWO

Luminous Light • 37

CHAPTER THREE

HU-man Wave • 51

CHAPTER FOUR

Evolutionary Body • 69

CHAPTER FIVE

Evolution Equals Revolution ◆ 87

Preface

During the soft transition from darkness to light, and light to darkness, for a brief period the planet's surface gains access to the thin veil between Third and Fourth Dimension. The Master Teachers group the first three dimensions— thought, feeling, and action—and define them as the *Earth Plane.* Saint Germain refers to this as "the plane of action." Our physical experience is inspired from higher planes of consciousness, referred to as the Fourth and Fifth Dimensions, and additional higher planes of consciousness.

The transition to Twilight Time is a momentary opening when your prayers, meditations, and decrees are assisted by your Spiritual Teachers and Guides. During these brief minutes the heavens literally open and humanity is spiritually strengthened and lifted. This is the most effective time to practice Violet Flame Decrees for your Ascension. According to the *I AM America Spiritual Teachings* sunrise is masculine and is mirrored in Saint Germain's piercing qualities of Alchemy, Transformation, and Transmutation. The sunset is feminine, and Kuan Yin is this period's parallel of feminine Mercy, Compassion, and Forgiveness. Both periods are advantageous and can be discernibly used for a specific focus or spiritual result.

The series of channeled lessons you are about to read were received by my wife, Lori Toye, in early 2010. By that time, I had been monitoring trance sessions for nearly twenty years and I have had the inordinate benefit to become personally acquainted with Saint Germain as a mentor, teacher, brother, and friend. Interestingly, throughout these series of sessions the Master of the Mighty Violet Flame casually refers to the breath technique taught in these discourses as, "the gift." I have no doubt that the breath technique taught in these lessons is the next generous step that further develops your practice of the Violet Flame. This technique connects the sacred, alchemic fire to every cell in your body through a rhythmic breath technique.

The breath is drawn through the Third Eye and travels to the heart in a slow inhale and exhale. As you practice you will notice a coolness in your breath that travels from the *Ajna Chakra* (Third Eye) to your *Anahata Chakra* (Heart Center). I suggest applying a cool cloth, or even an ice cube on your Third Eye as you begin the breath technique. Soon you will begin to sense the cool, tranquil stream of energy traveling to your Heart Center.

According to the Masters of the *I AM America Spiritual Teachings,* within the human heart resides the Eight-sided Cell of Perfection. The Eight-sided Cell of Perfection holds our innate divinity and contains the Threefold Flame of Love, Wisdom, and Power. The Twilight Breath initiates the duplication of this perfect cell. This process expands and develops your light bodies of Ascension. Apparently, the aspiring HUman descends from a genetic lineage associated with non-technical spiritual evolution. Undeniably, it is our destiny to progress and grow spiritually. We are uniquely integrated and spiritually joined as ONE with Mother Earth, nature, and creation. This is our perfect Oneness, the bedrock of what the Master Teachers refer to as Unana—Unity Consciousness.

Love, Wisdom, and Power are also known as the Pink, Yellow, and Blue Rays. These foundational Ray Forces embody the light and sound frequencies for the first three dimensions. This, too, correlates to the Archangels: Archangel Michael of the Blue Ray of Action and Power; Archangel Chamuel of the Pink Ray of Love and Feeling; Archangel Jophiel of the Yellow Ray of Wisdom and Thought. These Ray Forces are the unique metaphysical mechanics of the Eight-sided Cell of Perfection, and when used alongside the Twilight Breath simultaneously activate, harmonize, and develop your HU-man evolution.

Blessings on your HU-man journey,

Lenard Toye

CHAPTER ONE

Twilight Meditation
Saint Germain

Greetings Beloveds in that Mighty Violet Flame. I AM Saint Germain and I request permission to come forward.

Response: *Please Saint Germain, come forward. You are most welcome.*

There is still much work that is planned between us Dear ones, Dear hearts, as it has been some time since our last formal discourse. However, we have had many discussions, have we not, in the planes of the Fourth Dimension?

Response: "Yes, we have."

"REVIVES EVERY THOUGHT"

There is much that is happening upon the Earth Plane and Planet, much which I would love to give discourse about, instruction, and continued information. This would regard not only the Time of Change but also the transitional events which will lead mankind into the work of the mighty Golden Flame. Dear ones, as I've always instructed, it is important to bring forth that mighty Violet Flame in all of your activities. For you see, it is that flame that gives the most refreshing drink. It revives every thought and also reinvigorates the cells within the physical body. The Violet Flame, you see Dear ones, Dear hearts, also gives an impetus to raise the body, the intellect, the intelligence, the mind, the thoughts, the feelings, and the actions into the glory of the Ascension.

THE PATH OF LIGHT

You see Dear ones, the Ascension Process is one which raises all energies of the human condition into a new way of seeing things, into what we have always discussed is a new point of perception. However, it is often difficult to understand in your Earth Plane why it is so difficult to raise your energies into the higher vibrations of the Ascension. Ascension, as Dear Sananda has always said, is the free gift that is given to mankind at this time. There have many that have gone before you in this burst of light, in this burst of glory. However, very few indeed have been able to follow those upon this path of light. The path of light, you see Dear ones, is where a greater understanding of life in the fullness is given. The path of light is also a path, not only as the lighted stance, but also a light in consciousness . . . a light in perception . . . a light in your perspectives . . . a light in all of your feeling world and your action world.

LIGHT AND LIFE

This light, you see, will bear its own fruit. Many times it has been spoken, "the fruit that you bear." Dear ones, Dear hearts, it is important to keep your consciousness focused upon the light of Ascension, for the light of Ascension is, as I have stated, the glory of light, but primarily a glory of life. The Ascension is also the teaching that, not only is brought forward for your consciousness and spiritual awareness, but it is also a teaching that is held viscerally within the energies of the Golden Cities. The Golden Cities, you see, have been brought forward at this time for the evolution of mankind and the Earth Plane and Planet.

The Earth Plane and Planet, you see Dear ones, is also rising in its own light and life. The light and life of circumstance and the light and life of situation seem sometimes to be quite heavy; however, the Light of God, as we have always stated, Never, Never Fails. The light you see is consciousness. The light you see is intelligence. The light you see is energy in its purest form.

ARCHETYPES OF CONSCIOUSNESS

The Ascension, when you understand it in its fullness, is a teaching that is brought forward to unite, not only biological sciences and religious sciences, but it leads one into an understanding of the human psychology and the archetypes of consciousness. In your own archetypes of consciousness, you will begin to understand what holds you back and what can move you forward. For you see, indeed these archetypes have been a choosing, not only a psychological choosing of this lifetime, but also a choosing which is kept through the soul and its memory from lifetime after lifetime after lifetime.

SEEDS OF CONSCIOUSNESS

The Golden Cities will raise humanity into the lighted stance, into the glory of the New Times and into a greater understanding. It is true that there is much that is happening upon the Earth Plane and Planet in terms of societies, cultures, and the governmental structures; however, even these, Dear ones, must all raise in their vibration and energy to accommodate the new humanity. The new humanity is indeed the seed within you. Even these words, as we speak today between us, are seeds of a New Time and a new consciousness. Each new seed of consciousness, you see, must be watered carefully and tended so that it can grow and produce its fruit.

THE PITFALL OF GREED

So, understand Dear ones, I stand here now as your friend and elder Brother, a Brother who has tread the path before you and understands the great pitfalls that lie in front of the human condition. As we have stated so many times before in our teachings, one of the great pitfalls that stands in front of humanity is greed. There are many who do not understand what a terrible condition this brings, not only to your own psychology, but also brings an energy level to the condition of life and light itself.

You see Dear ones, it is not money that makes a man prosper, it is the light, the life, and the love that is shared among others. This indeed is the true prosperity of the true life, of the true ONE united in the Ascension consciousness. However, there are many who say they do not have enough and that there is not enough prosperity around them for them to enjoy. Of course, we have always given information on prosperity decrees and how to increase the activity of abundance to, in, and around you. However, one of the greatest pitfalls, again I will remind you, is of greed and the hoarding of material energies, which keep you and hold you back from this new fresh consciousness that lies in front of you. Before I proceed, are there questions?

Question: *Yes, could you define greed?*

FEAR FEEDS THE FIRES OF GREED

Greed, you see, is fear. Fear that has turned inside is a fear of an inability to accept light and life. Those who fear are in constant need of renewal of security. The security then surrounds the person in the form of greed. However, as we have stated so many times, money is not at the root of such greed. Greed, you see Dear ones, is a psychological problem. It is an archetype that exists in the consciousness. It is a fear that is impregnated through the animal consciousness. Of course the human is working to raise its energies of the Kundalini out of the animal consciousness; however, it is difficult, as many have come to understand, as greed is always associated with fear and fear feeds the fires of greed. Does this help?

Question: "Yes, it does. However, there is a difference between greed and having enough, the balance of having enough?"

You must understand Dear ones, Dear hearts, that when I speak in this manner, I speak of the energies that are gathered in the Astral Planes in the Fourth Dimension to raise you into the glory and light of the Ascension.

Response: *I understand.*

LIGHT, AWARENESS, AND VIBRATION

It is a matter of gathering about you, as an aggregate consciousness of light, the great light and life that permeates all the planes of conscious awareness and understanding of the human. For you see Dear ones, surrounding you even now, in this moment, there is enough abundance, radiance, energy, and light to fulfill any desire that you may dream . . . any desire that you may have thought of . . . any desire that you have placed, shall we say, in the apple, or heart, of yourself.

This energy and substance I referred to in many past teachings is the ability to precipitate [manifest]. However, Dear ones, it is only through your conscious awareness of the substance you may charge and then bring into actual manifestation, this manifestation happening through the conscious awareness of light. Light, when I speak in this manner, is a thought; it is a conscious awareness, a frequency, and a vibration. Each vibration, you see, carries within it, its own musical note and harmonizing effects.

FEAR HAS CONSCIOUSNESS

Those who engage in the energies of greed are indeed engaging at a harmonic of a lower vibrating energy, that not only can bring precipitation, but also vibrates primarily with fear. It is difficult, we understand, to let go of this fear condition, for the fear itself has many different levels of archetypal consciousness and thinking in the human. Perhaps it is more important that we focus on the removal of fear, just in your day to day activities. Of course it is true that the removal, out of your dietary regime, of all flesh substances of any animal who has a spine will begin to remove some of the cellular fear that resonates in vibration and energy as a harmonic to the animal consciousness.

TUBE OF LIGHT

However, it is important too, alongside the dietary requirements, that you also focus upon the Light of God that Never, Never Faileth. This light is the golden stream of life, light, and activity that pours from the mighty I AM Presence. Sometimes we refer to this as the silver cord. Sometimes we refer to this as the pulsating Tube of Light. It carries within it the resonant harmonic frequencies which will imbue your presence this day, right now, with more energy, focused attention, and life eternal. Dear ones, Dear hearts, the charging of this can be accomplished through many different manners. However, perhaps one of the most effective and efficient that I have found to aid in the Ascension Process is the use of meditation.

MEDITATION AT DUSK OR DAWN

It is true that meditation that is performed in the transitional times of twilight, dusk and dawn, is always the best. For you see Dear ones, Dear hearts, this is the moment when the busyness, or shall I say, the waking energies of humanity, or the sleeping energies of humanity throughout the world, are indeed lightened. This frequency of twilight, or this frequency of dawn, is indeed celebrated through the Beloved Archangels as the Violet Flame. There you will see the meeting of the two magnificent Ray forces expressed in a colorization as pink and blue. These are the meeting of the forces that also must quell and take command upon the

Earth Plane and Planet as the mighty Will in Action and the Love Eternal.

Meditation that is performed at either of these time periods is most effective in gathering this light substance about you. This light substance, you see, as you charge it about you, can take command at any moment. It is filled with the energies and impregnated with the focus of the mighty I AM Presence.

ASCENSION AND THE ACTIVITY OF THE GOLDEN FLAME

The I AM Presence is always connected to you Dear ones, Dear hearts, throughout your physical embodiment. Yes, it does indeed withdraw itself at the time of death, but that is only death from the Earth Plane. There are many who continue their process throughout the Fourth Dimension and onward, if they so choose, into the Ascension of the Fifth Dimension. These energies create, if you will, a portal that transports consciousness to another plane. From this plane of understanding and reality, the Ascension Process, through light, life, and love, is harmonized within the being and understood and qualified for activity. Dear ones, this is also known as the activity of the Golden Flame. The activity of the Golden Flame, you see Dear ones, as it travels throughout the dimensions is also the flame activity which will carry you into the Ascension. [1]

The Ascension, while it produces a withdrawal of the energies, such as the karmic energies and also dharmic energies of the Earth Plane, it also expands your awareness and understanding of the ONE life. The ONE life exists in, through, and around all conscious awareness and beings upon the Earth Plane and Planet. This ONE life permeates thoroughly the Third Dimension, the Second Dimension, and the First Dimension, but it extends itself even further on, into dimensions that the human now seeks to understand, the Fourth and Fifth Dimensions. Ascension,

---

1. See Appendix A: Gold Ray.

you see Dear ones, as Sananda has said so many times, is the gift, but mankind must carefully and artfully awaken these energies to be used.

The activity of the Golden Flame, when brought into meditation, or lighted to coalesce the energies about you, collects these energies within your light field. You may then take them into your conscious awareness and program them for manifestation. Now when I speak of manifestation, I am speaking of the manifestation of events, events that you may perceive and see yourself to have within the Earth Plane and Planet time frame. But it is also a manifestation of how you may see yourself, that is, in terms of archetypal thinking and conscious awareness. [2]

The activity of the Golden Flame, Dear one, is best achieved through this meditation technique. First focus upon the Third Eye and breathe within, filling the lungs slowly and carefully. It is an energy that travels first to the Heart Chakra, and as we have taught so many times before. There it radiates and begins to fill through that chakra.

[Editor's Note: One powerful breath technique, the Rhythmic Breath, used for regeneration and taking in various Ray forces, might be explored here In-breathing a Ray force to a count of eight (or six if just beginning this type of breath work); then holding the breath, Absorbing the Ray force to the same count; exhaling, focused upon Expanding the Ray force throughout the energy bodies to the same count; and then holding the breath out, Radiating (or Projecting) the Ray force to this same count. For this application, it would be In-breathing the Golden Flame through the Third Eye, Absorbing the Golden Flame into the heart; Expanding the Golden Flame throughout one's energy bodies; then Radiating the Golden Flame.]

---

2. See Appendix B: Lightfields of Ascension.

THE EIGHT-SIDED CELL OF PERFECTION

You see Dear one, Dear heart, the Eight-sided Cell of Perfection is activated, not only through certain types of breath work, but it is always activated through your conscious awareness. Just the understanding of its existence brings this Eight-sided Cell of Perfection into consciousness, into the ability to bring you into greater perfection and understanding of Ascension. As we have taught in many other discourses, Ascension indeed does travel through the dimensions. [3]

INTERACTION IN GOLDEN CITIES

In order to gain a greater awareness of Ascension, travel to Golden City Vortices. For you see, as we have taught so many times, there is a greater interaction in these areas that has been carefully planned and predicated for humanity at this most important time. There, Dear ones, Dear hearts, you can tune in to the Fourth Dimensional energies, not only of those of the Elemental and Devic Kingdoms, but you can contact to the Fourth Dimension and, especially through the various Adjutant Points, the many other Master Teachers that are present to guide and direct your process through the Ascension.

FEAR-BASED CONSCIOUSNESS

There are many other processes that I could explain to help you through the Ascension Process, but I would also like to talk more about greed. For you see, greed, Dear ones, Dear hearts, can be a pitfall. It is whenever you engage in any activity that is related to fear-based consciousness. Fear-based consciousness, you see, almost hinders, if you will, almost stops, if you will, the Ascension Process, because in that moment, the heart reverts into a more

---

3. See Appendix C: The Eight-sided Cell of Perfection through the Dimensions.

human-like activity and away from its understanding of the perfection that permeates at all times. Of course fear was given to the animal consciousness for the preservation of the species. However, as a human, it is the Divine Monad that is within an animal body and given the Eight-sided Cell of Divine Perfection to evolve and to grow through the process of liberation and Ascension. I sense your question.[4]

"WITHIN THE LIGHT"

Question: "Yes, you started with a breath technique, specifically through the Third Eye, bringing in the golden light into the heart. And you discussed how fear inhibits the Eight-sided Cell of Perfection. Are you referring to all forms of fear?"

Yes, Dear ones, Dear hearts, and as we know so well, the dark side, which exists still within the human, has perfected every form of fear that could possibly exist upon the Earth Plane and Planet. However, let us put our focus upon the Light of God that dwells within, the Light of God that lights the path of intelligence and awareness. Let us focus on the Light of God that Never, Never Faileth, for within the light are the answers. Within the light comes the peace that will pass all understanding. Within the light comes the access, not only to the Fourth Dimension, but initiates and continues your growth and awareness into the Ascension and liberation process.

BEAUTY

It is true that many have focused upon detachment as a way to evoke the use of perfection. The human condition, you see Dear ones, Dear heart, focuses not only upon detachment, but it is also delighted through beauty. The Ascension Process follows the path of beauty

---

4. *See Appendix D: Location of the Eight-sided Cell of Perfection within the Human Heart.*

in all things. Perhaps this is one of the best uses of the Ascension Process, to liberate the consciousness into the understanding of the archetypes of consciousness of the Fourth Dimension. For there, the path of beauty is always celebrated . . . there the path of beauty exists in harmony and cooperation. The breath itself allows, not only an expansion of this heart of perfection, but allows an expansion into the heart of awareness.

Be aware each day of each subtle nuance around you. This may be difficult, especially for those who have been taught that there is only a black or a white way of seeing things. However, within these levels of harshness there are the sweet nuances that carry cooperation and the path of beauty. Each delicate way that you can perceive a new circumstance or situation helps to expand your conscious awareness. Not only in meditation, carry this light throughout your day as the activity of the Golden Flame in all of the situations and circumstances. The expansion of awareness brings one into understanding the growth and beauty of the Ascension Process. As we become more aware of that which is reeling around us, we begin to embrace a more beautiful luminous life. This luminous life is as food to your soul. Questions?

Question: *It is then how we see it? The challenges can be fearful, or they can be something that we can rise to.*

It is not only how we see. It is also as we sense. It is also how we feel. It is also as we experience. And it is always as we take action.

ABUNDANCE

Question: *When we look at the overall economic picture that is very contrived in our world today, I am wondering how most of the planet will fair out?*

Please understand Dear one, Dear heart, that all life is also programmed to receive this luminous life and light. Take this unto the laboratory of self. Experiment with it yourself. See the response, how the human condition will respond to greed that is activated always by fear. And then give the choice of how human consciousness responds to abundance, which is activated by life and light. Take this unto yourself.

Question: *Yes indeed. I have some questions if you would be willing to receive these?*

I am always here to give assistance. For we see Dear ones, I am an elder Brother and above all, I am a friend, a friend who gives help and aid to those who seek an understanding from a different dimension, a different dimension of experience and action.

THE TRANSITION INTO FOURTH DIMENSION

Question: "We have a question from our friend Connor regarding his Mother's recent passing: Can you tell me how my mother Nancy is doing? My father wishes he could hear from her. Is there some message that you can convey from my mother to my father that will be uplifting for him? He remains skeptical but hopeful about realities beyond the Third Dimension."

It is hard for those who have been programmed in their consciousness to see life and light as hard and fast, as black or white. However, numerous times this Dear one has worked to make contact to receive information. Several times in the early morning, has he not felt someone gently tapping him on the shoulder? This is often one of the best ways for a Dear loved one to communicate with another Dear loved one after they have made their transition into the Fourth Dimension.

You see Dear ones, even though it seems as though death exists in its finality, it is not so, for the being moves on back to the Fourth Dimension and there begins their own preparation, a preparation, yes indeed, to return back to the Earth Plane to learn, to grow, and to experience. But also a time period is always spent in the planes of light and sound of the Fourth Dimension. This Dear one has not only been working with sound vibrations and the energy of the Green Ray, but is also in the process of preparation.

SUBTLE ENERGY

Sometimes a soul spends some time visiting other members of the family, working to comfort them and to assure them that life moves on in the eternal glory of the creation. In fact, this Dear one has moved several times towards the father to give grace and comfort. It is a programming, you see, again of subtlety and nuance. Questions?

Question: *Is there anything I can do to assist Connor, beyond sending the Violet Flame? How should I direct the Violet Flame to him?*

Perhaps teach him the simple meditation on the heart at sunrise and sunset, to gather these energies of subtle influence. This would then allow him to begin to feel these more subtle energies that exist and permeate, not only throughout the Third Dimension, but have their origins in Fourth and Fifth Dimensional consciousness.[5]

THE E-MOTION

Question: *Saint Germain, would you explain what is meant by the feeling side of life and how best to open it?*

---

5. See Appendix E, *The Twilight Breath of Luminous Light.*

The feeling side of life is often described as the e-motion. For those who have trouble understanding the emotional qualities of life, it is best to start by listening to music, music of any type that you enjoy. However, I prefer classical music because of the rhythms and patterns of nature that are present in all these and within the separate harmonies. Music, you see, raises one to feel and to understand the astral existence. This is perhaps one of the best places to start to begin to understand the energies of the astral level.

Art too, you see, and the path of beauty are other ways to raise energies into the e-motion and to understanding the balance of color and symmetry of form. All of those are brought to bring about a feeling, a sensation. Many humans, you see Dear ones, get blocked from moving into the emotions, not only by fear, but by over sensualizing their senses and indulging in addictive and nonproductive patterns. Dear ones, I hope that this gives some help.

THE VIOLET FLAME AND THE TEMPLE WITHIN

Question: *Connor has another question: I understand there is a temple dedicated to the Violet Flame. Would you discuss the temple, its purpose, its location, and how best to access it?*

Perhaps the mightiest of all temples of the Violet Flame is located within the altar of that great and mighty Cell of Perfection. However, in the histories of humanity, there have been several periods where temples of the Violet Flame have existed, not only in physical form, but in the ethereal Fifth Dimensional forms. The most powerful of these temples was present in the days of Atlantis, that which you know as the land of Poseidas. This of course today is located in present day Cuba. However, some remnants of it can still be felt as you walk on the beaches of Florida in the United Stated of America and the North American Continent. [6]

6. *See Appendix F: The Violet Flame.*

This mighty Violet Flame, you see Dear ones, was used as a transmuting fire and it grew in its use throughout many of the peoples at that time. It brought about, not only the transmuting of the animal consciousness, but allowed the growth of conscience among humanity at that time, the ability to choose from right, from wrong, and the ability to sense the subtle layers of energy.

Question: *Thank you. There are a couple more questions from Connor: I realize that immortality is really about embodying the I AM Presence. This is something that I am working on. Do you have further guidance for me?*

Work upon meditation of the Golden Flame.

And Dear ones, I suggest that we continue on a weekly basis with our discourse. For you see, we too then can build a continuous consciousness through this discourse and further dispensation of this work for I AM America, the land of those who can choose . . . the land of those, who through destiny, will unite again with the mighty Violet Flame. Om Manaya Pitaya, Hitaka. [I AM the Light of God, So Be It!]

Response: *Hitaka.*

CHAPTER TWO

Luminous Light
Saint Germain

Greetings Beloved chelas in that mighty Violet Flame. I AM Saint Germain and I stream forth on that mighty Violet Ray of Mercy, Compassion, and Forgiveness. As usual Dear hearts, Dear chelas of mine, I ask permission to come forth.

Response: *Please Saint Germain come forward. You are most welcome.*

Greetings Beloved students and chelas. Today we will continue our discourse upon the Luminous Light, that is, the light that builds within the Astral Plane and the astral body. This light, you see Dear ones Dear hearts, is also the light, as I stated in my past discourse, that is used to build the body for the Ascension. There are many upon the Earth Plane and Planet who requested this type of information and so I will continue in this instruction.

FOURTH DIMENSION AND EXPERIENCE WITHIN

In many past discourses, we have given information about the Golden City Vortices and how the Golden City Vortices can affect your light body and bring it into the Luminous Light. This happens, of course, first at the physical level. You see Dear ones, the Golden Cities themselves are filled with a type of energy, chi, or orgone, if you will. This energy is used to raise the physical body into a higher sensitivity, that is, to the first outreaches of the astral level, or what we also call and know as the Fourth Dimension. The first effects of this are felt in the physical body. As I have stated in many other discourses, the first thing that you can hear is a high pitched ring. This means that your resonant frequency, or your vibration, if you will, is entering into the first levels of the Fourth Dimension.[7]

This high pitched ring, you see, is very important for you to recognize. For you see, it is not something that you hear outside of you; it is an experience that is within you. This that you are hearing is the resonant frequency of your own energy field, of your vibration. Many times you may have noticed this high pitched ring, but thought it was something outside of you, an electromagnetic response. But indeed, it is within you. It is your own resonant frequency, resonant energy, that is responding to the outer environment. You have had an opportunity to tune within and to feel this resonant frequency. This energy, you see Dear ones, Dear hearts, is also related to the activation of the Eight-sided Cell of Perfection, that great desire that is within to achieve and know perfection.

DIET AND VIBRATION

The Eight-sided Cell of Perfection is also activated when one enters into the Golden City Vortices. Some will notice first, heart palpitations or a quickening, if you will, of your metabolism. Some will also feel heat or a sudden flush or energy rush cover the entire body. This too is part of the activation process. However, Dear ones, if you are having trouble feeling that frequency of energy when you enter into the Golden City Vortex, it is important then to stay on a pure vegetarian diet for approximately five days before entering into this type of work.

Now, when I talk about the vegetarian diet, I am talking of vegetables and grains only. It is important to eliminate animal products of all types. This also includes fish. For you see Dear ones, Dear hearts, anything that has a face, anything that has a spinal cord, must be eliminated from the diet, for this carries a type of resonant frequency which may hold you back from experiencing the awakening or the opening of the Eight-sided Cell of Perfection. Now, as I have stated in so many other past discourses as well, it is important to stay upon this type of diet as much as you can. But remember Dear ones, Dear hearts, to keep things always within balance, and remember always, that it is not so much what you put into your mouth, but what you speak with it.

ANIMAL CONSCIOUSNESS

The vibration and energy of the vegetarian diet removes the discordant thoughts, or shall we say, even the emotional body, the emotional residue that is often within the animal consciousness. These beloved companions of ours have been brought in, not only to experience their own karma and dharma upon the Earth Plane and Planet, but they have also been brought here to be as our companions. In a later discourse, if you so choose, I will bring forward more information regarding this.

The animal consciousness, you see Dear ones, is what the human has strived to overcome. Once this consciousness, which can be filled through the death process with the residue of fear does enter the body, it lowers its vibration. It takes approximately seventy-two hours for this energy and vibration to leave the body once it has been ingested. However, we like to add in this Lodge, an additional two full days to that. This ensures that all residue has passed through the body.

CITRUS AND THE GOLDEN RAY

Now, in other prior discourses as well, I have brought forward information upon Cellular Awakening and how one may use citrus juices in combinations to heighten your response to vibration. This is done of course through the work of the Gold Ray, which brings forward its energy and radiance through the maturation process of these fruits through sunlight. It is best of course always to use the citrus fruits that I have suggested before: grapefruit, orange, tangerine, and some lemons. For you see Dear ones, this is a type of rind that exists upon this fruit which allows a collection of this type of energy, the Golden Ray, to be brought forward in its full manifestation.[8]

This too can be used in a combination twenty-four hours before entering into a Golden City Vortex. This allows even a higher harmonic and a finer energy from the Great Central Sun, also known as the Galactic Center, to enter into the heart and allow these frequencies of energy to enjoin in their collective response to awaken the heart.

AWAKENING

The Adjutant Points, you see Dear ones, are also strategic points that have been brought forward at this time of the collective awakening. They allow, not only more beings of the Fourth Dimension to enter into the finer reaches of the Third Dimension, but also allow strategic points to be placed on Babajeran, the Earth Mother herself, to assist in her own awakening process. For you see, as I have stated before, the Earth Plane and Planet is also raising in vibration along with the HU-man. The HU-man, Dear ones, is your Divine Destiny. It is where you are going. It is indeed the goal for those who are on the path of awakening. The HU-man resonates to the higher human experience. The HU-man indeed is the God-man, who is working to awaken the light within, the luminous light body, and also applying and utilizing their force, power, and energy.

Life is not just limited to the Third Dimension, as many of you understand as aspirants on this path. Life is filled with subtleties and nuances, a many layered experience upon the Third Dimension. However, as one awakens within the heart, one will begin to understand the many nuances and subtleties that do exist beyond the Third Dimension. One begins to understand the frequency and energy of the Astral Plane and also the spiritual energy that can fill one

8. *See Appendix H: Golden Ray Diet.*

from the Fifth Dimension. These dimensions are all what are involved in building the Luminous Light. The Luminous Light indeed is the aggregate of all of these energy bodies coming together to serve the HU-man.

TELEPATHY

The HU-man also participates regularly in telepathy. This is the use of the timeless energy of the Fifth Dimension. It is true that much of this ability is honed in the Fourth Dimension and also utilized by the Beloved spirit beings, as we have discussed also, the gnomes, the salamanders, the undines, and the sylphs. They live upon this type of telepathic energy, one that can not be understood or contacted by a regular Third Dimensional human, but the HU-man is in constant contact and awareness.

Perhaps you have noted them scurrying about your home, or if you are out on a walk, you notice something flickering in the corner of your eye. They are always there Dear ones. They are part of the Luminous Life of which I speak. They participate always upon the energy of the Fourth Dimension, which plays its harmonic, not only with the Astral Plane, but also is interpenetrated from time to time with the energies of the Fifth Dimension. This is much in the same way that your Third Dimensional life, from time to time, glances upon Fourth Dimensional and Fifth Dimensional energies.

THE RADIANT ASCENSION

The HU-man's goal is to cultivate these energies and to bring them forward in their full glorious illumination, which culminates, of course Dear ones, Dear hearts, in the glory of the radiant Ascension. The Ascension, you see, is the process of obtaining the Luminous Light. This Luminous Light is present at all times for you to partake.

EARTH CHANGES

Now, I will continue with more information on the Golden City Vortices. There are many upon the Earth Plane and Planet who see the Golden City Vortices as an alternative to experiencing cataclysmic Earth Changes. Now I assure you, Dear ones, Dear hearts, the prophesies that have been given about the Earth Changes may happen, and please understand Dear ones, I place my emphasis on may. Have you not noted, throughout the twenty years of our relationship together, the many changes that have happened upon the Earth Plane and Planet, many of those things that we had talked about so many times. Is this not so?

Response: *Yes, it is.*

Not only are we now experiencing the beginning of Map One of the Six-Map Scenario, especially along the lines of global warming, we are experiencing many of the other changes, or shall we say, prophecies of life leading into the New Times and into the new paradigm. One of these of course is the economic blight that humanity is experiencing at this time. Many see this as a complete melt down, if you will, of a system, but this is a system that does not serve the HU-man.

THE UNRAVELING

Stand fast and stalwart, Dear ones, Dear chelas, students of mine. We only know and understand that this unraveling process is also being used at the higher levels to bring about a new sustainable system that will address the need and the economic climate for the New Times for the HU-man. The economic blight, you see Dear ones, may take up to twenty, perhaps even thirty years in order to stabilize itself and for the light of a New Day to come within it.

In the meantime, if you would like to stabilize your own economic position, I have always stated that natural resources are the best place to place your investments. Of course also, this includes precious minerals, and I will also add gemstones. Perhaps gold and certain gemstones are one of the best investments one may make at this time. For you see, they have the ability to hold and collect the higher frequency and energies that are needed to build the energy of the Luminous Light for the HU-man.[9]

CONNECTING HU-MAN EXPERIENCE

Now I will continue with more information regarding the Golden City Vortices. Upon five days of this fast, that is, removing all animal products from the diet, not only will you begin to notice upon entering the Golden City, a high frequency pitch, sound, or hum, you will also begin to notice a Oneship. First, you will notice a tingling in your physical skin. This tingling, or rush, is the beginning, not only of the opening of the heart, but the activation of the chakra centers upon the Kundalini. Some have often called these truth bumps and some call them goose bumps. However, we all know that this is a higher energy, a frequency that is connecting the HU-man experience to the life around it.

The Luminous Light and Luminous Life surround you at all times. However, many do not recognize or see it. Even now in this room, it is filled with many other forms of life that you have yet to recognize or understand. The developing HU-man begins to understand this light and life as it exists, and begins to harmonize their life with it, accepting their position in the Oneship. This frequency, or shall we say, wavelength of the ONE, is essential to calibrating the consciousness, which also then brings one into a greater understanding of the Fourth Dimensional life.

---

9. See Appendix I: Saint Germain on Economics and Nations.

ASTRAL LIGHT

Of course it is hard, in your work-a-day world, is it not, dealing with the daily pressures, the traffic, the noise, even that of interpersonal relationships? When one begins to understand that this is only just the backdrop to understanding the true luminosity that waits beyond in the glory of the Ascension, ascending to this new dimension will also bring, not only a feeling of Oneship, but also a difference in your sight. Many of you, I know, have already experienced this type of vision of the astral light. However, as you proceed into the Luminous Life and building the Ascension Body, one begins to notice, not only the light that surrounds your own body, but light that surrounds those who are closest to you.

FAMILY

It is true that those who live in one household begin to resonate to one frequency and they share, if you will, a collective light and life. This has been known in the Third Dimension as the family and while there is a connection to this light with the DNA and genetic coding, it is primarily affected by the resonant harmony and frequency that is held within a household. The family, you see Dear ones, Dear hearts, is one of the first steps to understanding the Luminous Light. For the family that you surround yourself with, the family that carries even your genetics, is all united in ONE, in the Oneship, in the HU-man's movement toward the Fourth Dimension.

ENTRANCE INTO THE GOLDEN CITY

The HU-man, you see Dear ones, Dear hearts, is not only the goal, the HU-man is a way of life. The HU-man respects life at all levels at all times. This is the code. Much awaits you in the glory and knowledge of this. I also suggest, in your entry into the Golden City Vortices, that you call upon

the mighty I AM and let this be your decree as you enter
each of the Adjutant Points:

> Mighty I AM Presence come forth
> in the Luminous Light and Life.

Let this be your decree as you enter the Star:

> Mighty I AM Presence,
> I call forth the Ascension in light and life.

Each one of these points, you see, is as sensitive as the
points upon your own body. You are connected as ONE. As
the Earth continues its Ascension Process and moves into
its higher energy, you too may contact her energy and use
it to assist your own process. As so many times we have
said in past discourses, we are ONE. Indeed, Dear Brothers,
Sisters, we are ONE. We are ONE family . . . we are ONE Light
. . . we are ONE Luminous Life. Questions?

THE HALLOWED FLAME

Question: *Yes, I do have questions regarding the Ascension. What
is the connection to the Unfed Flame in the heart and the Eight-
sided Cell of Perfection?*

The Unfed Flame is the spark of consciousness. It is
the Divine Intelligence that anchors the essence of the I
AM Presence into the physical body. This has also been
known as the Monad, as the masculine principle, as it has
existed as the "Father which art in Heaven." You are the
hallowed ONE. You see Dear ones, Dear hearts, the flame
sits upon the altar within the temple, the Eight-sided Cell
of Perfection. It surrounds this hallowed flame within its
serene cooperation and completed beauty. The Eight-sided
Cell of Perfection is the first manifestation into physical
form. The Eight-sided Cell of Perfection therefore carries
within it, a feminine quality. It allows itself then, through

this, to reproduce itself as one enters into greater resonant frequencies and harmonies into the Fourth Dimension.[10]

The Eight-sided Cell of Perfection then is critical and most important for the Ascension Process and I will add, that upon the Earth Plane and Planet at this time, there are many other circumstances or situations, if you will, that can hinder the duplication of the cells within the heart. Many of these chelas have begun to understand that these are deadly preservatives and chemicals that the dark force, if you will, have placed within your food chain. However, we will save that for yet another discourse. But I will also make this comment, that the energy in force of the Monad, that mighty Unfed Flame of Love, Wisdom, and Power, has the ability to transmute any discord, disharmony, and situations brought into the physical body. The Eight-sided Cell of Perfection holds the perfection and allows the duplication of the resonant frequencies of the Unfed Flame. Questions?

THE FOURFOLD FLAME

Question: *Can you ascend on one of the flames in the Unfed Flame or is it all three?*

All three, you see, represents an element and aspect of the Third Dimension. In past discourses, I also gave you some information upon the Fourfold Flame, which is given when one initiates their consciousness to the next level, into building the light bodies of Ascension. The Fourfold Flame of course will be highly responsible for bringing forth this mass attention into the energy of the HU-man. The Fourfold Flame, you see Dear ones, Dear hearts, will be held by many of the new children who are being born at this time and who will also come into the Earth Plane and Planet to raise its harmonic frequencies a thousand years into the period of Grace.

10. See Appendix J, *The Unfed Flame and Sacred Iconography.*

OPENING THE FEMININE

The Fourfold Flame, while carrying the primal energy and instincts of the Monad, evolves into a higher frequency and energy. It integrates, not only the aspects of the masculine principle, but also allows an opening into the feminine. This feminine energy, you see Dear ones, Dear hearts, is essential to understanding the Fourth Dimension. It opens the heart to a new level of awareness and recognizes the Oneship and joy of creation.

ABSORBING CHI

The Eight-sided Cell of Perfection indeed can be duplicated and replicated within the body. This is done of course through heightening the consciousness. As I gave in the last discourse a meditation upon absorbing the Luminous Light of twilight, this of course is the chi and energy of the transitional phases of dusk or dawn. As you have experienced yourself, these too can be used to build more frequency energy into the Luminous Light, into the Fourth Dimension, and the building of the light bodies. This too, however, builds the beginning of the Fourth Flame. [11]

ONESHIP AND UNANA

The Fourth Flame of Love, Wisdom, and Power is the flame of Oneship. This Oneship is critical and key in understanding the consciousness of Unana. Love, Wisdom, Power, and the ONE will catapult you into the Ascension Process. Indeed Dear hearts, it will and it shall.

THE NEW SOULS

There will be many who will be born upon the Earth Plane and Planet, not only coming in through the Golden City Vortices, but also coming in through the Swaddling Cloth,

---

11. See Appnedix K, The Fourfold Flame, page 00.

that area protected by the Beloved Mother Mary in Brazil. Those stalwart souls, coming from many other planets at this time, understand the power, energy, and love of the Oneship at this critical time in the history of the Earth. Questions?

Question: *Are some of these other souls part of the Galactic Federation?*

They come of course through the energies of the Galactic Web. You know, I have also given some information regarding this miraculous web. They come heralding like a cry form the darkness from the Earth to other planets of like vibration and consciousness. As Earth raises in its own Ascension Process through the energies, not only of the Golden City Vortices, but of each and every one of you individually and collectively, your light shines forward into the universe and calls forth an equal energy of like vibration to answer the call.

EVOLUTION AND THE LIGHT

Question: *I see, so in a certain sense, as the planet is going through its own Ascension, and we are physically very similar, then the planet would also have its own Unfed Flame?*

From the core of itself. So many times we have spoke of the core as a white light. It too is a Luminous Light and as the Earth takes this new flame, like a new strand of DNA, it comes into physical form where it evolves the flora and fauna that exists upon the Earth Plane and Planet. This too, you see, is not just a physical process. It must first start at the Fifth Dimension and matriculate downward from the Fourth and finally into the Third. That is why our discourse has come from the Fifth Dimension and we meet upon a plane on the Fourth Dimension. Right now, can you not hear that high-pitched frequency and energy in your ears?

Response: *I always hear that. It never leaves.*

ENERGY FOR ENERGY

This, you see, is the harmonic frequency. In the beginning, as I prepared to enter into this stewardship of information called I AM America, it was important to be prepared to receive the information. So again, as we came through those planes of energy, the Sixth, to the Fifth, to the Fourth Dimension, lowering our harmonic frequency to accommodate this information, you too had to heighten your energy. This has always been taught as energy for energy.

ASCENSION, ALIGNMENT, AND PURIFICATION

There is not one chela or student who will enter into the Ascension who will not seek through the process of alignment or purification. This is a process or course of heightening their own energy, of discarding what is no longer needed, and moving ahead in their path of dharma towards the Fourfold Flame. This Flame, you see Dear ones, is the Flame of Unana and united as ONE in the Ascension Process . . . yes, through the Eight-sided Cell of Perfection . . . yes, through the Adjutant Points and the Stars of Golden City Vortices . . . yes, through the Earth and her Ascension Process . . . leading us all on the ever present path to understanding greater unity through the Luminous Light and Life. Questions?

THE ENERGY BETWEEN

Response: *I have no further questions on this discourse.*

Continue on your practice of the meditation. It is important of course for you to capture at least twenty minutes of the energies of twilight. Proceed.

Response: "I have noted in my own meditation, that there is not only the stillness, but there also seems to be a slight separation between the light and the dark and at that time, this heightened energy that we are working to participate in seems to stream in."

That is the thin barrier sheath that exists between the higher levels of the Third Dimension and the lower harmonic vibration of the Fourth Dimension. That energy, you see Dear ones, is the energy that you collect and hold within that temple of consciousness, the Eight-sided Cell of Perfection. This feeds, not only the flame, but also allows more duplication and replication of the Cells of Perfection. This affects first the astral body and later of course you will have an effect upon the physical body.

Response: *I see. I have no further questions on this and will continue on with the discipline.*

So Be It. And now, unless if there are further questions, I shall take my leave from your density.

Response: *There are quite a few questions, but my sense is that I should hold them for another discourse, if that is all right with you.*

So Be It. As I say Dear ones, Dear hearts, in the Light of God that Never, Never Fails, that there will always be energy for energy. Om Manaya Pitaya, Hitaka.

Response: *Hitaka.*

CHAPTER THREE

HU-man Wave
Saint Germain

Greetings Beloved chelas in that mighty Violet Flame and that mighty Violet Fire. I AM Saint Germain and I request permission to come forward.

Response: *Please Saint Germain, come forward. You are most welcome.*

Dear ones, Dear hearts, it is important to always keep your focus upon the Violet Flame. For you see, the Violet Flame has the ability to lift your energy fields out of discord and disharmony. This transmuting fire and flame was brought long ago by the Lords of Venus to this planet to remove discordant energy from the animal body. The Violet Flame was brought to raise the animal consciousness (to human and) into the vibration of the HU-man.

HU-MAN CONSCIOUSNESS

The HU-man, you see Dear ones, Dear hearts, is the goal and the objective. For in achieving the consciousness of a HU-man, one then is able to enter into the consciousness and the energy of the Ascension. The HU-man resonates, not only at the Fourth Dimension, but at the Fifth, Sixth, and onward into the Seventh Dimension. Of course, the HU-man is the elevated body consciousness in the Earthly condition. But the HU-man is also a consciousness that is utilized to raise the body, the thoughts, the feelings, and the actions, raising the emotional body and of course the mental body. The thoughts, the feelings, and the actions of all of these are raised into, not only the energies of the Fourth Dimension, but into the energies of the Ascension.

KARMAS

As the body enters into the Ascension, one then is able to drop the karmas that are incurred upon the Earth Plane and Planet. You see Dear ones, it is the karma that holds one to the trials and the tribulations that may seem like hell itself in the Earth experience. The karmas, which are also based upon actions, may also be something that has been positive in your lifetime. Karmas, you see Dear ones, Dear hearts, contain within them the desire of the Source. However, as one uses desire to reach to a higher level of consciousness, one eventually, in the human consciousness, releases the desire and moves into the energy of the Fourfold Flame.

ASCENSION AND FIFTH DIMENSION

To activate into the Fourfold Flame, we have talked about the meditations of Luminous Light and also entering into the Eight-sided Cell of Perfection. However, Dear ones, Dear hearts, the Fourfold Flame is absolutely essential to be cultivated and used in order to enter into the Ascension work. The Ascension not only relieves you from those seemingly dutiful actions of the Earth Plane, but also allows you then to enter into the Fifth Dimension.

The Fifth Dimensional consciousness is where service of a new type is then taken up. This service, you see Dear ones, is a service that has been brought forward by many of the other Beloved Dear ones who have come forward to the Earth Plane and Planet to lift the consciousness of mankind. Many of these who have given this service have been known as the Avatars . . . have been know as the Adepts . . . have been know as the Great Masters of consciousness . . .

have been known as those wizards of the many cultures of the Earth Plane and Planet.[12]

THE FOURFOLD FLAME AND LOVE

However, Dear ones, Ascension also lifts one into the harmony of the spheres, and one begins to expand their consciousness to understand, not only one individualized level of consciousness, but also a higher consciousness. This higher consciousness we have spoken of as Unana, or the ONE. You see Dear ones, the Oneship is important to embrace in all of its qualities, for the Oneship leads one into the activity of the Fourfold Flame.

The Fourfold Flame is contained, yes indeed in the human body, but it is this Fourth Flame of activity that leads one into this higher level of vibrating consciousness. I know Dear ones, it is hard to imagine or understand the ONE, especially if you are in the limited consciousness of a Third Dimensional reality. However, perhaps the greatest way to understand and enter into the beginning phases of the Fourfold Flame is to experience love. For you see Dear ones, as it has been stated so many times, love is indeed the tie that binds each to one another. Love, yes too, is the Law of Sustainability, but above all, Dear ones, it is a Law of Allowing. Love allows each one to be perfectly whom they are. Love never judges. Love allows all to be and to exist as it is. Love, Dear ones, is also an attribute in a higher understanding of the Fourfold Flame.

DEVOTION

Now love, when it is understood from the energy of the Three-fold Flame, is known as devotion. To devotedly give oneself over to another is one of the highest actions of love. This is perhaps the union that two may seek on the Earthly planes as marriage, a partnering that happens of course

12. See Appendix L, *Levels of Mastery through the Eight-sided Cell of Perfection.*

through devotion. Devotion though, Dear ones, Dear hearts, is indeed an activity of unity, for the two become as ONE and from this opens into the understanding of the Fourfold Flame.

SONS OF HEAVEN

The Flame that came originally from the Lords of Venus has been cultivated upon the Earth Plane and Planet throughout many epics and time periods of history upon the Earth. The flame itself, as the Violet Flame, was also used in those temples of the mighty Amethyst Island, that island now know today as Cuba. This island though at one time was much larger. And many other Lords of Venus came directly and sought embodiment upon the Earth Plane and Planet. These are recorded in your present day Bible as those Sons of Heaven who came and united with the daughters of man. Some have referred to these Lords of Venus as the Anunnaki. However, they are not Dear ones. They were brought instead to help forge a higher consciousness for the HU-man, that would be realized, not only in the epic of the Aryan, but onward into the evolutionary phases of the souls upon Earth.

TRANSCENDING TO THE ONESHIP

One of the higher purposes of moving into the consciousness of Ascension, that is, Ascension defined as consciousness that is transmuting and transcending, is that the natural result of this transmuting and transcending consciousness leads one into a higher consciousness of the Earth. Of course again, as we all well know, this leads one to be able to put on a body at will. However, when one enters into the higher consciousness of Ascension, one no longer needs the physical body to understand, to know, and to feel this energy. Even at this moment, can you not feel the higher resonance frequency energy that is emitting from my own energy field?

Response: *Yes I can.*

This, you see, is brought forward, not only through the energy of the Ascension, that is, the transcending consciousness, but is also brought forward through the energy of Unity, that of the Oneship that we share. This Oneship, as you well know, we share as a soul group.

SEVENTH MANU

Now I shall share more information. The Seventh Manu, Dear ones, is coming forward at this time to raise the frequency and vibration of Earth. There are a few of these souls that are now entering into the Golden City Vortices and at this time, this is the only area where they are permitted to enter. There are a few, as I have stated in past discourses, that are also incarnating into the Swaddling Cloth. However, there will be those who will come forward in future generations about the whole population of the Earth. Many of these beloved Dear ones are entering into areas known as Adjutant Points. Why is this so? And why is this so important? Each of these points, Dear ones, Dear hearts, operates almost as if a higher energy center or chakra, if you will, of the Earth Plane and Planet.[13]

As Earth moves forward in her own evolution, ascending herself in her own transcendence, the souls that come in at this most important time, are coming forward, not only based upon the Law of Attraction, but also based upon those Laws of the Akashic Records. For you see Dear ones, many of them have been here upon the Earth Plane and Planet but ages and ages ago. They left this planetary stream and continued their evolution in other planets or galaxies of consciousness.

---

13. *See Appendix M, The Seventh Manu and the Swaddling Cloth.*

DNA AND THE FOURFOLD FLAME

The Fourfold Flame also activates within the HU-man certain DNA codings. These DNA codings resonate again with harmonics related to those genetics. Now again, please understand the emphasis of the HU-man and the human is very, very different indeed. The Earthly human body carries within it the DNA coding of many, many different types of galactic genetics. This was done, you see, to form the most perfect consciousness for the Earthly body. The Earthly body has evolved indeed from an animal consciousness, but it also was designed to accommodate the consciousness of many of those who would be incarnating upon the Earth Plane and Planet to serve the journey of their soul. All of these soul groups must come in through a Law of Attraction, and this Law of Attraction then serves indeed the Earth Plane and Planet.

GALACTIC FEDERATION

These levels of the Fourfold Flame resonate to different levels of the DNA coding. As the HU-man evolves in its use of the Fourfold Flame and the transmuting fire of the Violet Flame, leading into the transcendence of the Ascension, more and more purity will come forward from the Galactic Federation. Now, when I speak of the Galactic Federation, I'm speaking of those planets that have evolved into the higher planetary schemes of soul groups. This has been explained to you of course as lokas, or dimensions of higher experience.

Indeed, at any one time, any human in an Earthly body, if they so desire to the heart, can achieve the evolutionary process from any level of their being. However, there are those who will be coming forward, and for the best way to understand this and the best way that I can explain this, as purity or a higher resonant frequency. The lokas, levels, or dimensions, of these different Galactic Federation souls come forward at this time to begin to raise the energy of the Earth.

BELOVED BABAJERAN ASSISTS

It is true Dear ones, the Earth may likely go through a time of purification and a time of cleansing. This also happens to be one of the greatest opportunities for the soul to evolve and so many, many souls at this time are clamoring to enter the Earth Plane and Planet and yet all of this is by Divine Design. Each one of these souls that enters gives the opportunity, and is also presented the opportunity, to raise in vibration and also assist the Earth, as the Earth has come forward as Beloved Babajeran to give its assistance.

DNA AND THE GOLD RAY

Many have asked about the year 2012 and it is true that there was a beam that came from the Galactic Center at that time. This beam brought with it its own special, yet peculiar attributes. The attribute of this Galactic Beam allowed even a higher frequency of souls to come forward in their incarnation process and there were those who aligned to this Galactic Beam and also raised their energy to a new level of conscious understanding and awakening. This awakening of course we have discussed as the Cellular Awakening. However, now it calls forward for an enlightening of these strands of DNA.

The new souls coming forward will carry this new DNA coding, which also carries a resonant harmonic to the Golden Flame and the mighty Golden Ray. This leads humanity into a new and herald time, a time which will also bring forward a greater awakening of the heart within Brotherhood and an opportunity for world peace. Yet alongside this, comes great tribulation and trying as those upon the Earth Plane and Planet work to bring the frequency into a higher vibration.[14]

A BATTLE WITHIN

There is also a lower vibration, which brings forward its resistance. Sometimes this resistance is felt within. It becomes almost a battle of the light and the dark fighting within. And as we all know, one must put asunder that animal consciousness in order to embrace the Earthly experience and raise their consciousness into the HU-man, into the great God-man that resides within and without. The great God-man is the blessing at this time of awakening. The great God-man comes forward to show the true essence of the Earthly experience.

LUMINOUS LIGHT MEDITATION

Each of the Golden City Vortices assists every human being upon the Earth Plane and Planet to raise in vibration and energy. However, there may be those who do not have the opportunity to travel to one, and so for those who do not have this opportunity, it is important to understand the Luminous Light Meditation. The Luminous Light allows one then to also breathe in and take in, through harmonic vibration, the new energies that are present upon the Earth Plane and Planet.

As we stated last time, these energies are present at twilight. It is a type of orgone, or chi, as I have stated before, that penetrates the Earth Plane and Planet. It also causes a separation between the Third and Fourth Dimension, also between the Fourth and the Fifth Dimension and onward and onward. As these energies are taken into the energy fields, one then is able to raise in higher vibration and feel the true glory of the God-man, the HU-man within.

---

14. See Appendix N, *The Cellular Awakening.*

QUICKEN THE ENERGIES

However, it is my suggestion that this meditation is done and performed, not only in the Star of the Golden Cities, but for those who wish to have a quickening, perform the ceremony of the Luminous Light at Adjutant Points. This galactic energy is present at this moment. It is there for you to partake of and to use, if you will.

ARCHETYPAL CONSCIOUSNESS

The galactic energy heightened towards the year 2012. Now, why was that date so auspicious? It was because the collective consciousness grabbed hold of that date and saw it for what it was, each recognizing the opportunity to move out of darkness and into light. This speaks to the archetypal consciousness that is present in every man and woman and child upon the Earth Plane and Planet.

Of course the dark forces for the longest time have understood the archetypal consciousness and have used it in the mass media. However, it is used in its lower energies of the animal, primarily programming through fear, avarice, and greed. However, the archetypal energies are also present in the higher mind and that higher mind resonates with the energy of the Galactic Wave. Questions?[15]

DEVELOPING THE SOUL THROUGH LOVE, WISDOM, AND POWER

Question: *When you're speaking of that Galactic Wave, I am assuming it came from the Central Sun. Did it come through our own solar Sun and then to our planet and plane? Is that how it traveled?*

This energy of course triangulated, coming from the Galactic Center and arcing energy from Jupiter, Mars, and

15. See Appendix O, *Archetypal Knowledge.*

the solar sun. However, each person, through their own DNA coding, resonates to a different type of the energy as it comes forward, for their own spiritual growth and evolutionary process. Unfortunately, energy that comes more from that of Mars has a tendency to bring out more aggression in its lower form. However, in the higher form, brings forward great devotion towards spiritual application.

Energies that come through Jupiter, in their lower form, lead one more towards a fear and hoarding that is greed. In its higher form, it comes forward in an energy that seeks enlightenment of the mental body and places all in its harmonic understanding. Energies, of course, that come through the Sun, in its lower form, is what we have all known upon the Earth Plane and Planet as the male tyrant. When the sun, in its own evolution, is used in the higher form, it brings forward the birth of the feminine.

Now all of these are present in every man, woman, and child upon the Earth Plane and Planet in incarnation. However, one of these usually is more dominant. Each of these too corresponds to the Unfed Flame at this time. Love, Wisdom, and Power come forward in its higher understanding, Mars resonating to Love, Jupiter resonating to Wisdom, and the Sun resonating to Power. As they are all brought into their greater union, into their higher form, the Fourth Flame erupts, bursting within the heart, and leading one into the consciousness of Unana, into the ONE. Questions?

A WAVE OF CHANGE

Question: *Yes, what other affects is this beam having?*

It affected all upon the Earth Plane and Planet, all life, all flora and fauna, and many changes have happened as a result of this. The influence of this beam is still being felt right now. I have referred to it in both forms, as a beam and also as a wave, but perhaps the easiest way to understand it is like a wave, for it came forward much like the oceans and their tidal system, creeping upon you, waiting to reach its highest peak. This, of course, brings about an influence in your cultures and societies even at this moment.

As this wave came forward, it sought to change many things upon the Earth Plane and Planet. Primarily, it sought to change your economic systems and also many of your political systems. It also brought about sudden changes in your sciences, primarily the biological sciences, and how one understands life. Many of these things Dear ones, Dear hearts, you see are changing. These all carry an influence at this time.

THE INDIVIDUAL TO THE COLLECTIVE ONE

Question: *So you're saying that we are perceiving biology, our economy, and how our government functions in a different way since this wave completed its sweep through our planet and consciousness?*

Yes indeed, Dear ones, it brought forward the understanding of why governments need to become more regionalized. For you see, as this develops and one individualizes and understands the unique characteristics that each culture and society has at a regional basis to offer and to give, then they can move into a higher form of collective understanding. This, you see Dear ones, is the evolution of democracy, which seeks to understand the individual first, and then moves into the collective ONE. Of course this is a move away from the antiquated monarchies, which sought to understand the ONE first and then gave little to the individuals.

ONE AND EQUALITY

The challenge in democracy is to not move into individual concerns, however, evolve the individualized consciousness and understanding of these attributes at the archetypal level and move into the understanding of the ONE. It leads one into understanding that one country is the same as yet another. The ONE leads one into understanding equality.

"CONSCIOUSNESS IS HEATING"

The equal opportunity for energy and its resonant frequency and harmonies is given to all upon the Earth because of the Galactic Wave. Processing this wave has some difficulties upon the Earth Plane and Planet; it is even difficult for the Earth, Beloved Babajeran, to integrate herself. And this of course brings forward more earthquakes and brings forward more volcanic activity. This especially concerns those who have seen that life only exists for ONE, those that have brought forward changes in the ecosystem of the Earth. This you are now experiencing as global warming. And while most of this has been caused by man, there was also energy coming through this Galactic Wave which also influenced all of this; however, that influence is more in conscious understanding.

While some would say that indeed the Earth is heating, I would laugh and agree. Consciousness is heating. Consciousness is transcending. Consciousness is now growing among the masses. I have said so many times before, that you must have the eyes to see and the ears to hear to understand this work. This Galactic Wave of higher consciousness opens eyes and opens ears. So Be It.

Response: *So Be It.*

Do you have questions Dear one?

GALACTIC WAVE AND THE ELEMENTAL KINGDOM

Question: *I do. How is the Elemental Kingdom being affected?*

Each member of the Elemental Kingdom is participating also in this great shift and change. They of course too were affected by this Galactic Wave. And as the HU-man raises in its conscious understanding, there will be much more activity and interaction with these beloved beings of the Fourth Dimension. As one begins to understand their presence, one then will also interact in a different way. As I have prophesied, the Earth is entering a new way of being and thinking. This new way of being and thinking is in direct relationship to the HU-man and their understanding and love for the Elemental Kingdom.

MALTON AND DENASHA

Response: *So, in better understanding the Elemental Kingdom, our interaction will be taking a different direction.*

Not only will it take a different direction, it will also take a more visible form, for those who have the eyes to see and the ears to hear. The Golden City of Malton and also the Golden City of Denasha are allocated as some of the first areas upon the Earth, during this most important time, where one may become aware and contact those members of the Elemental Kingdom. They too contain their own hierarchy of spiritual evolution and cause and effect, and while it is somewhat similar to that of the HU-man evolutionary process, it is different in some ways. Their emotional bodies are formed a little differently than that of the HU-man and operate more closely at an instinctual level. Now this is not to confuse it with that of the Animal Kingdom, which operates through what is known as a group mind.[16]

---

16. See Appendix P, Devas and the Elemental Kingdom.

A HU-MAN CONNECTION

The Elementals too individualize themselves and sometimes these souls come in and enter into the HU-man planetary evolutionary scheme. During the time of the evolutionary process, where the body of the Earthling was developed, some of the DNA was used from certain members of these kingdoms. This has produced an affinity, you see, for the HU-man towards the Elemental Kingdom. Questions?

ECONOMIC EVOLUTION

Question: *Yes. In your last discussion, you talked about the economy. How is this changing?*

The economic situation upon the whole planet is evolving into a greater understanding of the need for sustainability. This of course is the Law of Love and Divine Activity. However, as I stated in my past discourse, that the use of precious minerals and gemstones will be used by those who understand this need for sustainability. Also, one will do best by investing in natural resources. Now when I say invest, I am not speaking of paper money, or paper investments, which mean very little for the times where we are all heading into Dear ones, Dear hearts.

The Time of Change is upon the Earth Plane and Planet and everything at this time will be reevaluated and evolved and transcended to a new level. Even your economies are ascending. Even your money, as you know it, is in an Ascension Process. All is moving to a higher level. Of course, what you are experiencing now, which some call as the downturn, or the crisis, or crash of the economy, is the dark side expressing in its lower form. Does this help?

Question: *It does. So when you're speaking of investments in natural resources that are not paper investments, what you are saying is to actually own farmland or something of that nature?*

This is true Dear ones. However, you know, we only make suggestions. We can never tell you what to do. You must make that choice indeed for yourself.

Response: *I see, so what you are just giving us, as you have said many times before, is the energetic reasoning of the direction that we are heading.*

It is true Dear ones, Dear hearts. For you see, as the HU-man moves into its higher understanding of the use of money, one then will begin to understand the true meaning of energy for energy. Energy for energy, as you move into higher states of awareness and consciousness, evolves its meaning, does it not, as you move throughout these dimensions of time and space?

GALACTIC WAVE AND THE ONE

Question: *Yes. The rules are different form one level of consciousness to another. Even though they have a seamless connection, they have a different understanding?*

As this Galactic Wave came forward, it beamed into the hearts of those who have the eyes to see and the ears to hear many, many changes. These changes are all in accordance to the Divine Plan and the Divine Will. The Earth indeed is ascending.

Response: *So, also this beam affected you and all other members of the Brotherhood and Sisterhood.*

Of course Dear one, it affects all of us, for we are all interconnected as ONE. We are indeed the consciousness of Unana.

Question: *I understand. Is there any immediate guidance you can give us for our Golden City community project?*

Focus always upon the ONE. Ask, does this decision serve the best and the highest good for all of those concerned? This will always give you your immediate answer at any time of trouble. I also suggest to always apply the Violet Flame in all of your prayers and applications for this project, for the Violet Flame will immediately remove any discord or disharmony and allow one to come into a higher understanding and consciousness alignment and attunement to the Galactic Wave.

THE NEW COMMUNITIES

During this time upon the Earth Plane and Planet, many communities such as these will arise. They come forward to give their service, not only to the Earth Plane and Planet in conscious awareness, but they also serve to bring a harmonization effect with the Earth. These, you see, are many important components of how the HU-man can now evolve and accept its new place in the ascending consciousness.

And as always Dear ones, call forth the assistance of Beloved El Morya, for he stands stalwart, ready to serve and to bring his wisdom of the Blue Ray to align to the Golden City of Gobean.

Response: "I have no further questions."

Then Dear ones, Dear hearts, I shall take my leave from your field and will return at the appointed time.

I AM a Being of Violet Fire.
The Earth is a purity of the Oneship's desire.
So Be It.

Response: *So Be It.*

Hitaka.

Response: *Hitaka.*

CHAPTER FOUR

Evolutionary Body
Saint Germain

Greetings Dear chelas, Beloveds. I AM Saint Germain and I stream forth on that Mighty Violet Ray of the consummate victory in the Ascension. For you see Dear ones, the Violet Ray is the mighty transmuting fire that can transmute any discord that causes that record in memory of all difficult karmas and all that will keep you from your victory in the Ascension of light, breath, and sound. Dear ones, before I continue our discourse, I request permission to come forward.

Response: *Please Saint Germain, come forward. You are most welcome.*

THE EVOLUTIONARY BODY AND FOURTH DIMENSION

The Evolutionary Body is most important, for you see Dear ones, the Evolutionary Body functions much like a subjective energy body; however, the Evolutionary Body has been brought forward at this time to assist in the Ascension Process.

There are many who have been following the Ascension work and have yet to have contact with the Fourth Dimension. The Fourth Dimension, as we have mentioned in many past discourses, is indeed a dimension of vibration, but is also a dimension where the Elemental Kingdom and the Deva Kingdom reside. Contact, you see Dear ones, with this kingdom of the beloved gnomes, sylphs, elementals, and undines, helps to calibrate the Ascension Body. But of most import, it begins to affect the human physiology, to understand the foundation in unity, Oneship, and the consciousness of Unana.

SPONSORED BY THE MASTER TEACHER

The Evolutionary Body, you see, is brought forward as an energy within the Fourth Dimension, so you can begin to assimilate and understand how light and sound frequencies work in this dimension of vibration. The Evolutionary Body is sponsored by a Guru, or a Master Teacher. Often times, even those who are in the unascended form use the Evolutionary Body; however, it is used in different context. We will keep it clear here that our definition of the Evolutionary Body is that used by an Ascended Master.

When a chela enters into the tutelage of an Ascended Master, this is often through the course of great desire. The chelas themselves have the desire to meet the Master, or begin on their own path of spiritual evolution which leads them to understand the negation of karma and the instigation of the liberation process. Of course it is important that the chela must have this great desire to meet the Master Teacher. We have discussed this information before as energy for energy.[17]

PLANE OF SYMPATHETIC RESONANCE

You see Dear ones, energy for energy is one of the most important concepts in the tutelage between a chela and a Guru. The Guru then becomes attracted to the light frequencies of the chela and the two meet on a plane of sympathetic resonance. And it is through this plane of sympathetic resonance that then the two begin their relationship and then this relationship comes and forges an energy that is known as an Evolutionary Body.

FROM DESIRE TO UNANA

This Evolutionary Body is indeed an energy body that comes forward, not only from the great desire within the chela, but it also comes forward from the desire of

---

17. See Appendix Q, Lineage of Gurus.

the Guru. Then two shall become as ONE. It is the first understanding of Unana. The same way as you meet the plane of the Elementals and Devas of the Fourth Dimension, in this same manner you also meet the Master Teacher. The Master Teacher then comes forward to lift you from your burdens and likewise, the chela lifts the Guru from their burdens.

BURDENS AND ENERGY FOR ENERGY

These burdens may be in the Earth Plane and Planet and the Third Dimension. They may also be burdens that happen in the Fourth, sometimes even in the Fifth Dimension. That is why chelas will become devoted to a certain particular teaching of a Guru, or even in some cases, of a certain religion. They begin to carry out a series of prayers, sometimes mantras, sometimes different ceremonies of all the different traditions, but then begin to give back as energy for energy. Sometimes these function on the Third Dimension, sometimes they function on the Fourth, and sometimes they function on the Fifth.

POWER OF BELIEF

This Evolutionary Body, functioning much like a subjective energy body, carries different collective beliefs. These beliefs are based upon different circumstances for the teaching that is involved. This Evolutionary Body, you see, is most important, for it contains within it the momentum of energy that can lead one into understanding, in this case through the Ascended Master teaching tradition, of the Ascension Process.

The Evolutionary Body is used much as a teacher would put on training wheels for a small child learning to ride a bicycle. The Evolutionary Body assists the chela in its beginning stages of understanding the beauty and freedom in Ascension. The Evolutionary Body can be detected first at the sixth layer of the energy field; for you see Dear ones,

Dear hearts, it also correlates to the sixth field of the Earth. This is also where collective beliefs are often held and the understanding that it is indeed the power of the belief that brings one into the ever-present understanding of experience. It is always in the beginning stages where one questions their beliefs; however, as Beloved El Morya has always said, choose, choose, and then choose again.

"SEE THE ONE"

The Ascension Process is indeed a liberation process. Of course it begins as a liberation of belief and then guides the chela, swiftly but surely, into the understanding of the ONE. The ONE exists in all things Dear one, Dear hearts. However, at times it is hard to see. In the moments of duality, as you swing from left to right, from feminine to masculine, from hot to cold, duality always carries its ever-present sway of illusion upon you. The Evolutionary Body allows you to see the ONE in all things. This Evolutionary Body of course allows you to have contact with the Fourth Dimension.

A SOFT GOLDEN GLOW

Now the Evolutionary Body, detected at the sixth layer of the energy fields, can also be seen as a soft glow of gold light haloed around the head. Some have understood this to be the mental body. Some have understood this to be the eighth layer of consciousness, based upon the Golden Ray. However, Dear ones, Dear hearts, as you are sponsored under this tutelage, I assure you it is a combination of contacts, that is, between the Guru and the chela.

ASSISTANCE OF THE ASCENDED MASTERS

Now there are those who say, is it not the time of the death of the Guru? And indeed it is Dear ones, Dear hearts, for it is important for you to always understand the deep wellspring of the inner Source. However, at this time, it is

also important that one seek and enter into th
relationship. For you see Dear ones, the Ascend
now come forward to bring their help and assista
most important time.

It has been long prophesied that a time would com
we would indeed reappear and this is the beginning o
this process. Some call this the reappearance of the Christ
Consciousness and indeed it is Dear ones, Dear hearts. The
Golden City Vortices were given some time ago, so that
those who have the eyes to see and the ears to hear could
begin to understand this ever present process of Ascension.
Now at this time, the Ascension Process is given to you as
a free gift, for indeed the Earth itself is in its infant stages
of the Ascension Process. This of course we have discussed
before in past teachings regarding the Galactic Wave, that
great golden beam, but now let us focus on the work and
the task at hand.

"THE SUBSTANCE OF THE ALCHEMIZING VIOLET FIRE"

I have given the information of the meditation at twilight
and of course this is also very important to continue with
great diligence. For what it does Dear ones, is it permeates
the body and the light body with a finer substance, a chi, if
you will, an orgone. This finer substance is best understood
as a molecular substance known as the Violet Flame and
Fire. Of course in the future, it will be known by other
names, but to keep this in its most perfect understanding
and simplest comprehension, this is how we shall refer to
it, as the substance of that mighty alchemizing Violet Fire.
This happens of course because of the transition of Light.
This is a time where the Violet Ray is available and can be
brought with even more efficiency into the system.

CEREMONIAL FIRE

Let us continue now upon the Evolutionary Body. The
Evolutionary Body is also seen with a bit of purple tinges

...g with the Golden Ray. This you will sense also as an electrical charge within the aura, sometimes even to the physical body itself. You have had the experiences of static electricity and it is similar to this, but you will also notice a small or faint scent of orgone as you begin in this tutelage with the Guru. It is also advised to use specific ceremonial fires, for these too will increase the tie between you and the Master Teacher. This can also be done at the time of twilight, where one builds a simple fire as a celebration of the Violet Flame.

INCREASE CONNECTION AND VIBRANCY

As you build this fire, you can chant always a simple mantra to the Violet Flame. As my student, chanting "Om Manaya Pitaya, Hitaka," is a visceral connection to me, and the Mighty I AM as your teacher. This increases our connection and vibrancy, along side your taking in the finer ethereal quality of the Violet Flame. This alchemization of the light field will indeed increase and it is important as you are in this process, to enter into the purification also of the body. The eating of animal products and flesh foods is not suggested for at least twenty-one days as you enter into this process with the Master Teacher. I have described and explained these reasons in past discourses and will not go at length at this time. However, I bring this up so you will bring it to the forefront of your understanding of the techniques involved.

MANY COME FORWARD

Now, there are many different ascended Master Teachers that are coming forward at this time to give this particular instruction of the Evolutionary Body. I, Dear Lord Sananda, Kuthumi, El Morya, Portia, Serapis Bey, and Beloved Soltec will all be available for those who wish to align their energies to ours. Also Beloved Mother Mary will be available for those whose belief systems will more carefully fit with hers. You see, we diversify for the different belief systems, as I mentioned before. There is a resonation, or shall we say, a harmony in the unity of consciousness with certain Ray forces. This you have known through astrology, but it is also something that is seen by those who can actually view the human aura and will see a certain color that is more dominant.

Now of course, all of the Seven Rays are present within an energy field, but there is always one that is more dominant. This of course has to do with the experiences that soul may be having in that particular lifetime and also, it will have a greater and finer harmonic with that of the soul group. Either one of these is a way to detect and determine what is the best for that person in terms of a specific Master Teacher.

There are also many ancillary teachers that will be coming forward at this time through the various Adjutant Points of the Golden City Vortices. I have mentioned only a handful of the Master Teachers that are available to give this information and discourse and there will be those who will also find other teachers that will speak of this in the mighty Ascension of Earth and her people. You see Dear ones, Dear hearts, we spent many years giving you the information regarding the possibility of changes upon the Earth Plane and indeed you are living in that time.[18]

EARTH IS ASCENDING

You will see many more catastrophic Earth Changes; however, as we place the importance upon the Ascension work, this will help nullify many of the occurrences of these and to eliminate the suffering in the Earth Plane. As we have stated before, the Earth herself, in her evolution, is now moving forward. Earth indeed is ascending and

18. See Appendix R, Adjutant Points of a Golden City.

Dear ones, you too shall come along with her. Now before I continue on more information of the Evolutionary Body, do you have questions?

Response: *I will reserve questions until you're complete with your discourse.*

ACCELERATION IN THE ASTRAL PLANE

The Evolutionary Body will also have an impact upon the Astral Plane. For you see, some of its attachment does adhere through the astral body and continue into the causal plane. At night, you many notice that you will have many different dreams, some of them connected, some of them not. The Evolutionary Body allows for an acceleration within the Astral Plane. That is, because of the connection to the Guru, to the Master Teacher, an acceleration of karma is allowed to occur in the Astral Plane. In past dispensations, much of the karmas were acted out upon the Earth Plane and Planet.

BEFORE YOU SLEEP

Now as we move through this acceleration, much of this great demand, as you will always know as cause and effect, will be lifted by the Guru into the Astral Plane. This can lead some of you to have nightmares and extreme situations at night. Now, I will remind you, that if you focus upon the Twilight Breath, it will also allow development of the Third Eye, and simultaneously, opening the Heart Chakra. This, if it is done before sleep at night, will allow some of these traumatic events to lessen and you will be able to enter into the higher levels of the Astral Plane where these karmas can be worked out in their finer order. Questions?

Response: *Considering some of the dreams, I would say that makes a lot of sense regarding working out the karma. So what you are basically saying is that those dreams are occurring at other dimensions.*

ALCHEMY IN THE ASTRAL PLANE

The Master Teachers lift the energy body, you see Dear ones, to this level where the cause and effect is taken from the Earth Plane and Planet. Now, it is important to understand that while there is a lifting of karma, there is not an amelioration of karma. Some may take the amelioration of karma into the physical plane and use this, not only through the fire of Alchemy, the mighty Violet Flame, but you can also, through the physical fire itself, open up the doorway to the Master Teacher to burn the fires of Alchemy of these karmas into the Astral Plane.

Question: *I am a little confused on your actual definition of lifting. It sounds to me like the karmas still exist, but the opportunity to transmute them through the use of the Violet Flame is what now becomes present?*

THE EVOLUTIONARY BODY

This is so Dear ones. The lifting of karma, means the lifting of certain karmas away from the field of action, so that they many be experienced at the actual level. This, of course, can eliminate some of the suffering on the Earth Plane and Planet, especially at this time as the Earth is shifting in her own evolutionary process. She too, has her own Evolutionary Body. This of course has been stimulated by the Galactic Center, the Great Central Sun, through the Galactic Beam. The Earth, you see, as she heaves and shoves in a different movement of tectonic plates and volcanic explosions of the different atmospheric and climatic changes that will be seen in this great period of change, is also the movement of her own karma to new levels of comprehension and understanding.

It is the lifting, you see, of this veil of karma as it moves from the physical plane to the Astral Plane. That is why the Evolutionary Body is so important to understand and to access. The Evolutionary Body also contains with it, its own consciousness, you see. This consciousness then is able to understand, in the unity of all things, the who, the what, the when, the where, and the why. All of these are the natural questions of the human. This consciousness, you see, also contains with it the impenetrable connection and the indelible connection to the Master Teacher. It is protected and held in the heart, that holy of holies, from one Eight-sided Cell of Perfection onward to the next.

We have explained this before, the perfection mirrors, yet again, but more perfection. This consciousness, you see Dear ones, also contains with it its own Akashic Record. This allows one then to enter into this higher state of knowledge. Now when I say higher, I say this only from your perspective, from the Third Dimension to the Fourth. The Third is not any higher or lower than the Fourth, but indeed the human sees it this way and I give this only for your understanding. However, this Evolutionary Body contains within it the consciousness of the eyes to see and the ears to hear.

TEN AND TWENTYFOLD

Now it is important, if you wish to perform several of these techniques in Adjutant Points of the Golden Cities, you will increase the efficiency of these techniques tenfold. If there are those who have the eyes to see and ears to hear, who wish to enter into the Stars of Golden City Vortices, it will again increase the efficiency of these techniques twentyfold. However, it is important that you align your energy to that great Master Teacher, whomever you choose and whomever they choose. Questions?

EFFORT

Question: *Yes. So this opportunity existing for us to transmute our karmas without them being in the physical plane, is there still energy for energy for transmutation?*

It is always energy for energy Dear ones; for you see, even though there is this great dispensation of the teaching and healing of the masses by the Ascended Masters, one must always, in the physical plane, make that important effort.

ASCENSION AND COSMOLOGY

Question: *I see. So as the planet is going through its own transition into Ascension, would it be a reasonable question to ask if the other planets in our solar system are ascended?*

Some of them are. As I have explained before, and as you well know, there is a cosmology that affects all of the planets. Some of them have these different lokas, or dimensions, where life is ever present and yet, in some of the other dimensions, it is not yet developed, or the life that does now exist in Third Dimensions is negligible.

Response: *I see. Well, that answers that question.*

MIGRATION PATTERN FOR THE EVOLUTIONARY BODY

Now, I would like to also give another technique of how to develop the Evolutionary Body. It requires, of course, a diligent heart and one must, with complete honesty to self, begin to resonate in energy and vibration to the Master Teacher of your choice. Of course you can work with any Golden City Vortex, but it is important to choose a Golden City Vortex that resonates to that Master Teacher that you have chosen to lead you into the initiatory processes.[19]

19. See Appendix S, *Spiritual Pilgrimage and Migratory Patterns.*

It is suggested then, that you go to each of the Adjutant Points. Start first on the outer layers. Travel first, starting in the Southern Door and move from the South to West, from the West to North, and end in the Eastern Door, and enter again from the Eastern Door of friendship over to the Star of glory. Then proceed again. Start again in the Southern Door with the innermost point, and travel again from South to West, West to North, North to East, and enter again into the Star. Complete this process as often as is needed until you begin to feel the growth of the Evolutionary Body. Of course there are many other byproducts of the growth of the Evolutionary Body; however, I shall be available to assist you as we start and initiate this process. Questions?

Question: *Is this a physical travel?*

It is always a physical travel Dear ones. It starts of course upon the physical plane. It enters then into the astral levels and from the astral, to that great causal body, where unity and the harmony of all exists. That is the reason, Dear ones, for the purpose of the Golden Cities at this most important time. It is indeed the Time of Change. It is a Time of Change for humanity and a Time of Change of choice.

DIFFERENCE FROM POINT TO POINT

Question: *Is it possible to just focus on one specific Adjutant Point and visit that?*

It is possible. However, there is a subtle difference from point to point, and each of these penetrates the energy bodies with a certain element of chi. Of course it always available in the Twilight Meditation. For those who are more sensitive to energy, they will feel this immediately upon entrance into the point. However, there will be those that it is harder for them to achieve this.

BEGINNING THE BREATH

For those who are beginning the formation of the Evolutionary Body, travel to these points and stay for a minimum of seven days, but no longer, Dear ones, and then move to the next point. Later, one can stay for up to twelve days. However, there may be those who will feel the instant integrity of the energy at that specific point in less than eight hours. It is different for every situation and circumstance. It is also highly suggested, as one enters into this initiatory process, that one has also forged that great connection to the I AM, to the Presence within, and also forged their connection to their Guru, to their Master Teacher.

Question: *The specific visitation for either eight hours or seven days or up to twelve days, really is to energize each individual person at each Adjutant Point and for them to do this breath technique of the Ascension Process?*

This is true Dear ones, Dear hearts. However, for those who cannot attend to the Golden Cities, it is important to focus upon the Twilight Breath and to build their fires, not only their fires within the physical plane, but the fire within and form the indelible connection to their teacher for the growth of the Evolutionary Body. Questions?

"FORGE THE CONNECTION"

Question: *Is this something that can be done in a group or is this done better as an individual or a couple, going to each of these points?*

It makes no difference. It is about the desire within the heart as always, to forge and form an indelible connection to the mighty God within.

Response: *I understand.*

Questions?

Response: *No, I don't have any more questions regarding this process. I will have to think about it more.*

I am available for further discourse upon this topic.

Question: *Did you wish to continue?*

I am available for your open questions.

Question: *Well, then could I ask a couple of questions that have been sent in?*

Proceed Dear one.

MASCULINE, FEMININE, AND THE HU-MAN

Question: *Thank you. One question is from Connor: in some of my recent meditations and energy work, I have had the experience, placing my hands over my heart, that the feeling of Divine Love is facilitated. Is this my imagination or can you give me an understanding of what is taking place when I have experienced this?*

When one places the right hand over the heart, in this instance, it activates the masculine energy, not only the masculine energies within the body's energetic system, but also a connection to the archetypal mind of the Divine Father. When one places the left hand over the heart, in this same technique, it activates, not only the feminine currents with the energy systems of the body, but also opens to the feminine principal, the Divine Archetype within. These of course are two of the most instantly recognizable concepts.

Now, when we move into the HU-man, I always ask for the left hand over the heart and to hold the right hand out. The right hand out, you see, not only can receive the energy of the evolutionary wave, that mighty Golden Beam and Golden Ray, but also one begins to feel and initiate the contact with the Evolutionary Body. Of course the left hand over the heart activates the Divine Feminine within and the grand intuition. This I have outlined in the map of the Eight-sided Cell of Perfection.

SCIENCE OF EXPERIENCE

Of course it is always a question, is it not, is it imagination or is it experience? Perhaps it is understood that in the beginning stages, it is a little of both. Yet as one moves deeper into the knowledge and begins to understand some of the science behind this, they will realize that indeed it is not only an exact science but an exact experience. Questions?

FROM HUMAN TO HU-MAN

Question: *Also from Connor: Sometimes in my meditation with the Violet Flame I feel parts of my body twitching and when I bring up energy from the Earth, it seems most active when I imagine the Violet Flame intensely swirling around me. Can you give me some understanding of these sensations?*

This may have to do with experiencing the energies of Mother Earth. You see, there are the experiences of Mother Earth that happen just in the body. These are the everyday Third Dimensional experiences of walking upon the Earth, breathing the air, just the everyday normal experiences of the human. However, the HU-man encounters experiences of the Earth as a Cosmic Being, the Beloved Babajeran. This also entails understanding her own thought, feeling, and emotion, and as they perhaps relate to your own.

There is also an understanding and taking in of the great Akashic Record; this of course coming from that grand mind, the mental body of Babajeran herself. However, these experiences are common with the developing chela and I would suggest for a discipline of the mind, to keep the body as quiet as possible, even though this can be difficult in the beginning stages. For keeping the body quiet will allow then an understanding and detection of the more subtle overtones. This of course, these great nuances, is where the joys lie. Questions?

Question: *I would also like to know, are there different aspects of the Violet Flame that can be used for different results and purposes?*

Perhaps the best way to understand it is, that there are different applications of the Violet Flame in any given situation. Of course today, I have given yet several new applications of the Violet Flame and how it can be used for the growth of the Evolutionary Body. Questions?

FACING EVIL AND PERSONAL FEARS

Question: *Yes, I have another set of questions. One is regarding chemtrails that seem to be in our atmosphere. Can you give us some information on this?*

Of course, as I have stated before, the Earth is going through this great Ascension Process and humanity too is making the choice to move beyond in its evolutionary course. This causes much polarization of light and darkness, of what is right and what is wrong. These of course are questions of morality that are still part of that great dual polarization. The chemtrails, you see Dear one, have been brought forward at this time based in, as we have always known, that great evil which is greed.

There is always that which wishes to control the masses, always that which wishes to have more and more power. The chemtrails, you see Dear ones, Dear hearts, are also part of the end times that we are experiencing upon the Earth Plane and Planet. However, continue in your effort to forge that indelible connection with the Guru within and the Guru without. This will help to calm you and to stabilize your fears.

AWARENESS IS PROTECTION

Question: *Is there a process or protection regarding this or transmutation?*

Awareness of course is always the best protection, awareness in all things Dear ones, Dear hearts. It is also important that as we move in our technique of the Evolutionary Body, the karmas are taken out of the physical plane and moved into the astral level where they can be more swiftly dealt with. I hope I have given you the information to understand.

MASTER KUTHUMI AND LADY NADA

Question: *I am assuming the Elemental Kingdom is also assisting, not only in the planetary transformation, but in ours. Is there anything that we can do to help to assist them?*

Beloved Kuthumi and the great Lady Master Nada are giving their assistance right now, through the Gold and the Ruby Rays, to assist the Elemental and Devic Kingdoms to move into their higher course of evolution. If one feels aligned to such work, they can align their energies to these great Master Teachers, where they can receive further instructions.[20]

Response: *I see.*

---

20. *See Appendix T, Master Kuthumi and Lady Nada.*

However, Dear ones, Dear hearts, use of the Violet Flame at all times can calm any situation and open a thousand doors.

Response: *I understand and as you have instructed before, the Violet Flame is even more effective at the twilight of sunrise and sunset.*

And at these hours of twilight, can you not feel these beloved beings of the Fourth Dimension dancing at your feet?[21]

Response: *Yes.*

I shall take my leave from your physical plane and shall return again at your next appointment.

Response: *Thank you.*

> I AM a being of Violet Fire,
> I AM the freedom of all-seeing desire.
> So Be It.

Response: *So Be It.*

Hitaka.

Response: *Hitaka.*

---

21. See Appendix U, *The Science of Twilight.*

CHAPTER FIVE

Evolution Equals Revolution
Saint Germain

Greetings Beloveds in that mighty Violet Flame. I AM Saint Germain and I stream forth on that Seventh Ray of Alchemy and Transformation. As usual Dear ones, Dear Hearts, I request permission to come forward into your energy fields.

Response: *Please Saint Germain, come forward. You are most welcome.*

THE SHIFT

Dear ones, there is still much work for us upon this Earth Plane and Planet. For you see, it is a time of shifting and changing, not only on the Earth but also in the spiritual fields of the Earth Planet. You've always known this to be the energy fields of Mother Earth, Beloved Babajeran. We refer to it sometimes as energy fields, sometimes as light fields. It is important to understand that it is, overall, a change in the spiritual essence of Mother Earth herself. This of course brings forward a big change within humanity and humanity must come forward now in its new evolution and revolution.

WORLDWIDE EARTH CHANGES

As the Earth Plane and Planet shifts, there will be many changes upon the Earth. This of course I've spoken about before in many different types of prophecies. There will be changes that will happen to the West Coast of the United States; many changes that will happen to the West Coast of

South America; many changes that we will see in the State of Alaska; many changes that will happen on the small islands of Japan.

Indeed, there will be many changes throughout the whole world and specifically, we will see many changes within Europe. The water there, you see Dear ones, Dear Hearts, will rise to heights that we will no longer see Europe as it once was. There will be many changes that will happen as a result of global warming. Of course, there will also be many changes that will happen in Africa and also in Australia.

CHANGE AND GROWTH

There will be great winds in India and also several more tidal waves (tsunamis) which will come throughout the Indian Ocean. These are all things that are prophesied to happen Dear ones, Dear Hearts. These prophecies of Earth Changes, you see, are not only designed to allow the Earth to release energy and to move into her own evolution and revolutionary stage, but also each change changes the heart of humanity and allows humanity to grow at a collective level, to open the heart of love to compassion, mercy, and forgiveness. Of course, there are those who ask "Why is it that we must go through so much strife in order to begin to understand the heart of love?"

FORGIVENESS, COMPASSION, AND LOVE

Dear ones, Dear hearts, in this time of Kali Yuga, pain seems to be the only way that opens the heart to forgiveness and to compassion. It seems as though humanity, in this time period, responds better to this as a spiritual technique. However, those who understand the difference, those who have the willing hands and the open heart, move into forgiveness, move into the heart of love now. Move Dear ones into the higher mind that awaits all of you. This Dear ones, we have spoken of many times before as that mighty Galactic Wave, that golden beam that is coming from the Great Central Sun. This of course is moving humanity forward into its greater evolution and greater understanding.

This is allowing, yes, the development of a greater understanding of compassion among the masses and opening the heart of love. It is also forging a deeper connection to the Earth, to Beloved Babajeran, and many can understand and feel the Earth as it heaves asunder.

UNITY AND ONESHIP

Dear ones, Dear Hearts, it is also important to move into an adept understanding of the Violet Flame. For that might Violet Flame of Mercy, Compassion, and Forgiveness allows one to transmute difficult karmas at this time. It keeps the consciousness out of polarization and moves it towards the ONE, Unana. This too is a result of these times. As we enter into a greater light in this time of Kali Yuga, we shall see a time of the lessening of polarization and many more will be able to enter into that greater understanding of unity and the Oneship.

INCREASE OF GALACTIC LIGHT

This evolutionary wave will allow the gross body of humanity to be lifted yet into a new state. This new state of understanding will allow a greater respect for spiritual knowledge and also, it can and will increase lifetimes, that is, the duration of the life itself. This is also due to the infusion of galactic light, which in the beginning stages, as we entered into this Time of Transition was functioning at a difference of anywhere between half a percent to one percent. As we moved towards the year 2012, we saw an increase of anywhere between five to six percent. However, those who are willing to apply the past teachings of the

Twilight Meditation and growth of the Evolutionary Body, can see an increase of this Galactic Light into their energy fields of up to fifteen, twenty, and even thirty percent.[22]

REVOLUTION OF LIGHT AND SOUND

Of course, this is also contingent upon the connection to the Master Teacher and how one is enabled to uplift their karmas to the Astral Plane, where that Master Teacher can ameliorate and destroy those karmas forever upon the Earth Plane and Planet, within the Third Dimension. This of course is all the process of spiritual liberation. It is not only an Ascension Process for the physical body, it is an Ascension Process for the soul. For the soul, you see Dear ones, Dear Hearts, in its own journey and sojourn, is moving on, moving on into the higher fields of light and sound frequencies where it can better express itself and continue in its own evolution and revolution. When I say revolution, you see Dear ones, this is indeed a revolution of light. It is a revolution of sound.

This Time of the Golden Age and the great Galactic Beam is a time of a revolution of the heart, where the heart may open to ONE consciousness and that ONE consciousness open to greater compassion and unity of people. Perhaps humanity will see an ending of the time of strife and war upon the Earth Plane and Planet. Perhaps during this time, we will see an ending of the great strife upon the Earth Plane and Planet that causes the horrific wind patterns and weather patterns and the famines that starve so many.

THE PERFECT CELL

But let us keep our attention upon the soul and the Alchemy within, the great Eight-sided Cell of Perfection as the Unfed Flame of Love, Wisdom, Power, and now Unity, in its fourfold evolution and revolution, moves into its greater understanding and application.

22. See Appendix V, The Golden Age of Kali Yuga.

"PEARL OF GREAT PRICE"

In our last teaching upon the Evolutionary Body, I gave more information about how the chela enters into this precious lineage with the Guru or Master Teacher. This of course is the pearl of great price. It is of course one of the greatest relationships that can exist for the soul in this lifetime. For this allows the soul to move in its greater evolution and journey. It also puts an ending to the revolutions of lifetime after lifetime after lifetime upon the Earth Plane and Planet. And the soul is lifted into the glory of the Ascension that is the physical Ascension. As energies are moved onward into the light body, the spectrum of light and sound energies are available then to lift the soul into greater comprehension and the wonderment of life.

"TEND THAT PRECIOUS FIRE"

You see Dear ones, lifetime after lifetime, it is a better journey, is it not? Lifetime after lifetime, the struggles, the joys, the great dreams, the great hopes and wishes, and also the great disappointments and the tragedies, all of these are part of the human condition. It is time now Dear ones, for us to focus upon what we can change and the thing that we can change within our self is always our desire for liberation. There are many who desire liberation, but yet will not apply or put the work and effort that is necessary and essential to achieve it. Why is this so? Because within them yet, that desire, that great flame within, is yet to be lit. It is important always to tend that precious fire, to keep that ember ready at any time, so it may burst forward into the Flame of Unity.

The fire of desire, in its evolved understanding, leads one into the liberation process. And as I stated in my last discourse upon the Evolutionary Body, it is indeed this fire within the heart, that light and sound frequency that attracts the correct Master Teacher, who can, in their own resonate frequencies and sympathetic harmonies, lift that soul, that precious beam of light into the journey of liberation. The journey of liberation leads one into a different understanding and we will see many, many changes that will happen to that course of time.

LETTING GO AND MOVING FORWARD

There will be those other friendships, family members, brothers and sisters, sons and daughters who may fall to the wayside as you enter into the liberation process. This of course was taught by the greatest of all teachers, Jesus Sananda, where he said "The two shall stand side by side and then one may no longer be." This of course is the process of letting go and moving forward. Dear ones, Dear hearts, when the fire is lit within the heart, one enters into a very specific course of understanding and one enters into a very narrow path that leads one, not only to the heart of desire, but beyond into their final liberation. This of course, as I have said, is always achieved with the assistance of a Master Teacher. This union, which is built upon the bonds of trust, is evermore important as we enter into these days and times.

ALIGNING TO A MASTER TEACHER

In these last days, as we exist upon the Earth Plane, isn't that true Dear ones, how you feel so much polarization, you feel so much duality? You exist one day in happiness, the next day in sorrow, moving back and forth, plummeting from side to side. It is of course the Master Teacher, when he or she comes forward in their understanding of the law supreme, who then is able to even out your energy fields, assist your light frequencies. This is why I have always asked for you to align yourself to the Master Teacher that you feel the greatest harmonic resonance towards.

It is important now for you to do the choosing, to light that flame within the heart and to choose the Master Teacher that best fits your resonance frequency and harmonies. Dear ones, I bring this discourse forward for those who have yet to make that choosing. For those who yet yearn within the heart to attend to the Ascension. Of course, as we know Dear ones, Dear hearts, you have long been aligned as my chelas, as my students and pupils. Dear one, before I proceed with more information upon the Evolutionary Body, are there any questions?

Question: *Yes, I have a question. In aligning to a Master Teacher, there will be those who will hear this discourse in far off lands. The Master Teachers that you have already previously given us, are there others that can be added to this list?*

MANY WILL COME

There will be many that will come. Of course, as we have discussed, there will be those who will teach in the Adjutant Points of the Golden City Vortices. I mentioned the major ones because perhaps they are easier to understand in terms of their archetypal energy and their force and power. It is important Dear ones, Dear Hearts, to understand this and I will give you some guidelines. For those who resonate to Beloved Sananda or to Beloved Mary, those are the chelas and pupils who resonate more to the heart of love. To those who resonate to Beloved El Morya and somewhat to myself, those are the pupils who resonate more to energy as power and the achievement of that energy through detachment and forgiveness.[23]

Those who resonate also to Beloved Sananda and to Beloved Soltec and to some degree Beloved Serapis Bey are those who pursue life through a path of healing and see that healing leads one into greater levels of liberation. This of course involves many who have embraced life through the biologic sciences. These are perhaps some of the students who must have proof and those of you who must have proof, almighty experience, these are perhaps some of

23. *See Appendix W, Ascended Masters of the I AM America Teachings.*

the better Master Teachers to align your energy and force with.

There are those upon the Earth Plane and Planet who see light through a much more simple approach and resonate in great harmony to the Earth Plane and Planet, to the Beloved Devas and Elemental Kingdoms. These of course will resonate in their great heart of compassion to Master Kuthumi. Lady Nada also sometimes falls within this category. These are also the students who may resonate more to the idea of the law that exist, as it does within the Earth Plane and Planet. Christians, Christianity, and those that came along side of it, that demand an eye for an eye, a tooth for a tooth, resonate more in a harmonic with this type of energy. However these Master Teacher can take this and evolve it to a new level.

"EVOLUTION BECOMES REVOLUTION"

As I stated before in this discourse, evolution becomes revolution. This also means a higher revolution within the body, a higher revolving of the light bodies. For you see Dear ones, Dear Hearts, your light bodies are revolving around your physical body. This of course happens at certain rates of spin and we have discussed this rate of spin in past discourse. This higher evolution becomes a new revolution and this revolving arc of spin allows one then to enter into the higher levels of consciousness that reside of course in the astral and causal planes.

Now, these are just some suggestions and there will be many more Master Teachers who will come forward and make themselves known to those who light that great fire of desire within the heart, for those who pursue the Ascension and the liberation process. Questions?

A NEW WAY

Question: *Are there certain Master Teachers that will be available specifically for those in Europe and Asia and Africa and South America?*

All of these Master Teachers are available for all upon the Earth Plane and all cultures and societies. There's no limitation at all Dear ones, Dear Hearts, no economic limitation, no social limitation, no cultural limitation. They are all available Dear ones, Dear Hearts, and are willing to serve. However, if a chela is in the process of choosing, sometimes it is best to visit specific Golden Cities that are aligned to certain Ray Forces and Master Teachers. There, one maybe able to take in the energy and understand the subtlety and nuance that it presents.

There will be many other Masters that will come forward at this time to give their assistance, that is, Masters upon the Earth Plane, those who have yet to achieve the Ascension, and they will give their great teaching and healing among the masses. However, for those who wish to achieve the Ascension, it is best to follow the light within the heart and to achieve a connection to a Master Teacher, one who is ascended, without a physical body, upon the spiritual planes. There are many teachings that will come forward at this time, in the next twenty to thirty years. These of course will lift humanity to a new way of seeing, a new way of living, and a new way of being. This we have always referred to as the New Time.

POLITICAL AND ECONOMIC CHANGE

We will see many changes that will happen in the United States. Right now, a great polarization happens among the masses, politically and governmentally. However, there will come a time where this will not be so. As humanity moves more towards a collective understanding and the unity of consciousness, not only along civil rights, but also in the right to know themselves within, this too will bring many changes and we will then see a more regionalization of governments, societies, and cultures. Of course, we will see some breakdowns economically, but this Dear ones, Dear hearts, will only allow a greater evolution spiritually.

EARTH CHANGES AND SPIRITUAL ENERGY

We will also see many changes in terms of weather patterns and many changes that will happen because of the Earth Changes themselves. This of course brings again a heightened spiritual energy that will lead many towards the path of liberation. Questions?

Question: *Truly the path of liberation is a choice, but unless you understand that this choice actually exists, how are you to make it? Many people are so caught in their conflicts and beliefs that they are not even aware of such a choice. Isn't it a very small percentage?*

"TIDAL WAVE OF CONSCIOUSNESS"

Indeed it is, but a small group of dedicated and stalwart chelas can make all the difference for the masses. This of course is one of the rules of collective consciousness. It is not so much of the quantity but more about the quality. It is about the fire that burns within and, if that fire is carefully tended, and if that fire is carefully focused, this of course is the great evolution and revolution I speak of. The Evolutionary Body brings about a whole revolution upon the Earth Plane and Planet. This revolution extends beyond the Earth and leads on into other planetary streams, lokas, and expressions, as I have spoken of in past discourse. This of course brings a total sense of a tidal wave of consciousness throughout the galaxy.

INTERCONNECTED GALACTIC WEB AND ONE

And in the same way that the Great Central Sun sends out its evolutionary wave as a Galactic Beam to the Earth at this most important time, the Earth is responding and sending out her own beam of conscious light. And this has its own effect upon the planetary schemes of lesser consciousness. Dear one, this of course, as you have understood, is the web of life and the Galactic Web is only an extension of this precious life force. All is interconnected as ONE and, as you move in your human consciousness towards this greater understanding of unity, you will indeed begin to understand the most important evolution and revolution that is affront. Questions?

"HU-MANS YOU SHALL BE"

Question: *It is a revolution, not a political or governmental though. It is a revolution of where we focus our consciousness, is it not?*

It is a revolution of kindness . . . it is a revolution of compassion . . . it is an evolution of unity. Let us all join together in the evolution and revolution that moves humanity beyond polarization and into the great understanding of the heart of ONE. HU-mans, you all are Dear ones, Dear Hearts. HU-mans you shall be. So Be It.

Response: *So Be It.*

Now, if you have any questions, please proceed.

EL MORYA: WARRIOR OF THE BLUE STAR

Question: *The only question I have is, do you have any immediate guidance for our Golden City community project?*

As always Dear ones, Dear hearts, that work must come forward from Beloved El Morya. He has many specific guidelines that he can give to help you achieve this. First however, align your heart and mind to Beloved El Morya. He of course is that great warrior of the Blue Star. Originally El Morya, you see Dear ones, as a soul came from the planet of Mercury. However from this course and his entrance upon the Earth Plane and Planet, he began to understand how the great will that is choice and the perseverance to achieve God perfection were indeed of his greatest interest. This was the great fire that burned within his heart and of course his many Master Teachers, including Sananda and Sanat Kumara, assisted him along this path.

LIGHT THE FIRE

It is important Dear one, that you align your energy to him. For this alignment process I will suggest this, travel to each of the outer Adjutant Points and light the physical fire at twilight and there align your heart and your will to the focus of the mighty Vortex of Gobean. There you will feel the essence and the whisper of his voice within. There you will gain the insight, the knowledge, the intuition and the great desire within. Perhaps of all of these, the fire within is the most important, for it is not only as we have stated, the unity of the causes of love, wisdom, and power, it is the unity of manifestation which then brings this to the physical plane. I hope this has been of some help.

Response: *It is. I have no further questions.*

Then I shall take my leave from your physical plane. In love, for the evolution and the revolution of humanity, I AM Saint Germain. Hitaka.

Response: *Hitaka.*

Spiritual Lineage of the Violet Flame

The teachings of the Violet Flame, as taught in the work of I AM America, come through the Goddess of Compassion and Mercy Kuan Yin. She holds the feminine aspects of the flame, which are Compassion, Mercy, Forgiveness, and Peace. Her work with the Violet Flame is well documented in the history of Ascended Master teachings, and it is said that the altar of the etheric Temple of Mercy holds the flame in a Lotus Cup. She became Saint Germain's teacher of the Sacred Fire in the inner realms, and he carried the masculine aspect of the flame into human activity through Purification, Alchemy, and Transmutation. One of the best means to attract the beneficent activities of the Violet Flame is through the use of decrees and invocation. However, you can meditate on the flame, visualize the flame, and receive its transmuting energies like "the light of a thousand Suns," radiant and vibrant as the first day that the Elohim Arcturus and Diana drew it forth from our solar Sun at the creation of the Earth. Whatever form, each time you use the Violet Flame, these two Master Teachers hold you in the loving arms of its action and power.

The following is an invocation for the Violet Flame to be used at sunrise or sunset. It is utilized while experiencing the visible change of night to day, and day to night. In fact, if you observe the horizon at these times, you will witness light transitioning from pinks to blues, and then a subtle violet strip adorning the sky. We have used this invocation for years in varying scenes and circumstances, overlooking lakes, rivers, mountaintops, deserts, and prairies; in huddled traffic and busy streets; with groups of students or sitting with a friend; but more commonly alone in our home or office, with a glint of soft light streaming from a window. The result is always the same: a calm, centering force of stillness. We call it *the Space*.

Invocation of the Violet Flame for Sunrise and Sunset
I invoke the Violet Flame to come forth in the name of I AM that I AM,
To the Creative Force of all the realms of all the Universes, the Alpha, the Omega, the Beginning, and the End,
To the Great Cosmic Beings and Torch Bearers of all the realms of all the Universes,
And the Brotherhoods and Sisterhoods of Breath, Sound, and Light, who honor this Violet Flame that comes forth from the Ray of Divine Love—the Pink Ray, and the Ray of Divine Will—the Blue Ray of all Eternal Truths.

I invoke the Violet Flame to come forth in the name of I AM that I AM!
Mighty Violet Flame, stream forth from the Heart of the Central Logos, the Mighty Great Central Sun! Stream in, through, and around me.

(Then insert other prayers and/or decrees for the Violet Flame.)

Glossary

Absolute Harmony: Order and peace permeate throughout.

Age of Cooperation: The age humanity is currently being prepared to enter; it occurs simultaneously with the "Time of Change."

Akashic Records: The recorded history of all created things from time immemorial, and constructed with the fifth cosmic element: ether.

Akhenaten: The ancient king of Egypt (1388 BC) embraced the unfolding consciousness of the ONE, which culturally replaced the polytheistic religion of his Kingdom. A pioneer of monotheistic religion, Akhenaten embraced the Christ Consciousness and some esoteric historians view him as a spiritual forerunner who led the way for the incarnation of Jesus Christ. According to the Master Teachers, Akhenaten is one of the prior lifetimes attributed to Ascended Master Serapis Bey.

Alchemy: A hidden yet transformative and sacred science which bridges the world of chemistry and metallurgy with the spiritual worlds of Mastery and Ascension Process.

Alignment: Balance.

Ascended Master: Once an ordinary human, an Ascended Master has undergone a spiritual transformation over many lifetimes. He or she has Mastered the lower planes—mental, emotional, and physical—to unite with his or her God-Self or I AM Presence. An Ascended Master is freed from the Wheel of Karma. He or she moves forward in spiritual evolution beyond this planet; however, an Ascended Master remains attentive to the spiritual well-being of humanity, inspiring and serving the Earth's spiritual growth and evolution.

Ascension: A process of Mastering thoughts, feelings, and actions that balance positive and negative karmas. It allows entry to a higher state of consciousness and frees a person from the need to reincarnate on the lower Earthly planes or lokas of experience. Ascension is the process of spiritual liberation, also known as moksha.

Ascension Process: The Ascension Process, according to Saint Germain, gathers the energies of the individual chakras and expands their energy through the heart. The Law of Love calibrates the energy fields (aura) to Zero Point—a physical and philosophical viewpoint of neutrality. From there, the subtle and fine tuning of the light bodies is effectuated through the higher chakras, sequentially including the Throat Chakra, the Third Eye Chakra, and finally the Crown Chakra. Zero Point is key in this process and it is here that the energies of all past lives are brought to psychological and physical (karmic) balance. Then the initiate is able to withdraw their light bodies from the physical plane into the Astral Light of the Fourth Dimension. The Ascension Process may take several lifetimes to complete and the beginning stages are defined through the arduous process of obtaining self-knowledge, the acceptance of the conscious immortality of the soul, and the use of Alchemy through the Violet Flame. Intermediate stages may manifest the anomalies of Dimensional Acceleration, Vibrational Shifting, Cellular Awakening and Acceleration, and contact with the Fourth Dimension. Use of the Gold Ray at this level accelerates the liberation process and unites the individual with soul mates and their beloved Twin Ray. Later stages of Ascension include the transfiguration of light bodies and Fifth Dimensional contact through the super-senses as the magnificent Seamless Garment manifests its light. It is claimed that the Golden Cities assist the

Ascension Process at every stage of development. According to the Master Teachers diet and fasting will also aid the Ascension Process at various phases.

Ascension Valley: According to the I AM America Prophecies, Ascended Masters appear in physical form in the Golden City Vortices during and after a prophesied twenty-year period. At that time, Mass Ascensions occur in the Golden Cities, at the Golden City Star locations, and in select geophysical locations around the world, which are hosted by the complimentary energies of Mother Earth. A model of this geophysical location is Ascension Valley, located in the Shalahah Vortex. The energy of Ascension Valley prepares students to integrate their light bodies and spiritual consciousness into the Oneship, the divinity within, and further prepares the body, mind, and spirit to experience and travel into the New Dimensions.

Astral Body: This subtle light body contains our feelings, desires, and emotions and exists as an intermediate light body between the physical body and the Causal Body (Mental Body). According to the Master Teachers we enter the Astral Plane through our Astral Body when we sleep, and many dreams and visions are experiences in this Plane of vibrant color and sensation. Through spiritual development the Astral Body strengthens, and the luminosity of its light is often detected in the physical plane. A spiritual adept may have the ability to consciously leave their physical body while traveling in their Astral Body. The Astral Body or Astral Plane has various levels of evolution, and is the heavenly abode where the soul resides after the disintegration of the physical body. The Astral Body is also known to esoteric scholars as the Body Double, the Desire Body, and the Emotional Body.

At-One-Ment: The spiritual practice and state of Unity. This spiritual ideal is philosophically affirmed through the recognition of humanity's innate divinity, equality, and human connection to ONE source of creation. This results in the At-ONE-ment, and the advanced practitioner morphs into a Step-down Transformer of the Seven Rays of Light and Sound as an expression of beauty and creation. The At-ONE-ment facilitates the consciousness of Unana.

Aura: The subtle energy field of luminous light that surrounds the human body.

Axiotonal Bodies: Light bodies of the Human Aura defined by magnetic energy lines, similar to acupuncture lines on the human body and lei-lines on Mother Earth. It is claimed Axiotonal Lines connect our human biology to resonating star systems within our galaxy, affecting human chemistry and genetic change.

Babajeran: A name for the Earth Mother that means, "grandmother rejoicing."

Belief: A conviction or opinion of trust based on insufficient evidence or reality. This confidence may be based on alleged facts without positive knowledge, direct experience, or proof. According to the Master Teachers, beliefs may be negative, positive, or both. Often the unchallenged nature of beliefs form the nucleus of Co-creative activity. The spectrum of individual and collective beliefs can vary from innocent gullibility to unwavering religious faith and conviction.

Blue Flame: The activity of the Blue Ray, based upon the activation of the individual will, manifests the qualities of truth, power, determination, and diligence in human endeavors. The Blue Flame is associated with the transformation of our individual choices, and its inherent processes align the individual will to the Divine Will through the HUman qualities of detachment, steadiness, calm, harmony, and God-protection.

Blue Ray: A Ray is a perceptible light and sound frequency, and the Blue Ray not only resonates with the color blue, but is identified with the qualities of steadiness, calm, perseverance, transformation, harmony, diligence, determination, austerity, protection, humility, truthfulness, and self-negation. It forms one-third of the Unfed Flame within the heart—the Blue Ray of God Power, which nourishes the spiritual unfoldment of the human into the HU-man. Use of the Violet Flame evokes the Blue Ray into action throughout the light bodies, where the Blue Ray clarifies intentions and assists the alignment of the Will. In Ascended Master teachings the Blue Ray is alleged to have played a major role in the physical manifestation of the Earth's first Golden City—Shamballa and six of fifty-one Golden Cities emanate the Blue Ray's peaceful, yet piercing frequencies. The Blue Ray is esoterically linked to the planet Saturn, the development of the Will, the ancient Lemurian Civilization, the Archangel Michael, the Elohim Hercules, the Master Teacher El Morya, and the Eastern Doors of all Golden Cities.

Breathwork: The conscious, spiritual application of breath, often accompanied by visualization and meditation forms the nexus of Breathwork. Ascended Master teachings often incorporate various breathing techniques to activate and integrate Ray Forces in the Human Aura and light bodies.

Cause and effect: Every action causes an event, which is the consequence or result of the first. This law is often referred to as karma—or the sixth Hermetic Law.

Cellular Awakening: A spiritual initiation activated by the Master Teachers Saint Germain and Kuthumi. Through this process the physical body is accelerated at the cellular level, preparing consciousness to recognize and receive instruction from the Fourth Dimension. Supplemental teachings on the Cellular Awakening claim this process assists the spiritual student to assimilate the higher frequencies and energies now available on Earth. Realizing the Cellular

Awakening can ameliorate catastrophic Earth Change and initiate consciousness into the ONE through the realization of devotion, compassion, Brotherhood and the Universal Heart.

Chakra: Sanskrit for wheel. Seven spinning wheels of human-bioenergy centers stacked from the base of the spine to the top of the head.

Chamber of the Heart: The sacred location of the Eight-sided Cell of Perfection, in the human heart. This site is surrounded by a mandala of energy: the Unfed Flame of love, wisdom, and power.

Chela: Disciple.

Chohan: Another word for Lord.

Christ Consciousness: A level of consciousness that unites both feminine and masculine energies and produces the innocence and purity of the I AM. Its energies heal, enlighten, and transform every negative human condition and pave the way for the realization of the divine HU-man.

Closure of Understanding: The completion and release of a Karmic lesson.

Co-creation: Creating with the God Source.

Compassion: An attribute of the Violet Flame is the sympathetic understanding of the suffering of another.

Conscience: The internal recognition of right and wrong in regard to one's actions and motives.

Consciousness: Awakening to one's own existence, sensations, and cognitions.

Conscious Immortality: Awareness, acceptance, and knowledge of the immortal, spiritual soul.

Cup: A symbol of neutrality and grace. The Ascended Masters often refer to our human body as a Cup filled with our thoughts and feelings.

Desire: Of the source; the ninth of Twelve Jurisdictions and states the heart's desire is the source of creation.

Deva: Shining one or being of light.

Dharma: Purpose.

Divine Cell: The Eight-sided Cell of Perfection.

Divine Complement: Each Ascended Master, Divine Being, and Archangel is alleged to be paired with a divine complement of energy. Each divine pair manifests and streams energies into the corporeal worlds through the Hermetic Law of Gender. Hence, one is masculine in quality, while the other is feminine. Similar to a Twin Flame, Divine Complements differ in that they are ascended and purposely divide their efforts to assist Earth and unascended humanity. In the higher realms they are ideally ONE energy, and serve upon one individualized Ray Force.

Dvapara Yuga: The Bronze Period of the cycle of the yugas when fifty to twenty-five percent light from the Galactic Center is available on Earth. During the last Puranic Dvapara Yuga it is alleged that the fabled continent and culture of Atlantis existed.

Dwarf Sun: A companion Sun that orbits with our Solar Sun and has no luminosity of its own. Astrologers speculate its juxtaposition between the Earth and our Sun obstructs, and therefore controls, the flow of this important galactic energy to Earth.

Eight-sided Cell of Perfection: An atomic cell located in the human heart. It is associated with all aspects of perfection and contains and maintains a visceral connection with the Godhead.

Elemental Kingdom: A kingdom comprising an invisible, subhuman group of creatures who act as counterparts to visible nature on Earth.

El Morya: Ascended Master of the Blue Ray, associated with the development of the will.

Emanation: To flow out, issue, or proceed as from a source or origin; especially the path of a Ray as it travels from the Great Central Sun.

Energy Balancing: Also known as Energy Work, Energy Balancing is a healing technique applied by a trained practitioner who balances the Chakra System of an individual through hands-on-healing and energetic adjustment of the energy fields and light bodies.

Energy for energy: To understand this spiritual principle, one must remember Isaac Newton's Third Law of Motion: for every action there is an equal and opposite reaction. However, while energies may be equal, their forms often vary. The Ascended Masters often use this phrase to remind chelas to properly compensate others to avoid karmic retribution; and repayment may take many different forms.

Ever Present Now: Time as a continuous, unencumbered flow without past or future.

Fifth Dimension: A spiritual dimension of cause, associated with thoughts, visions, and aspirations. This is the dimension of the Ascended Masters and the Archetypes of Evolution, the city of Shamballa, and the templates of all Golden Cities.

First Spiritual Body: A light body that forms through the merging of both the Astral and Causal Bodies and allows fluid experience with the spiritual planes. This light body incites the Ascension Process. It is not bound to time or physical laws.

Fourth Dimension: A dimension of vibration associated with telepathy, psychic ability, and the dream world. This is the dimension of the Elemental Kingdom and the development of the super senses.

Freedom Star: The Earth's future prophesied name.

Galactic Center: The great Sun of our galaxy, around which all of its solar systems rotate. The Galactic Center Sun is also known in Ascended Master Teachings as the Great Central Sun, which is the origin of the Seven Rays of Light and Sound on Earth. In Vedic tradition it is known as Brahma, which is the creative force or navel of Vishnu. This great Sun emanates spiritual light that determines life and intelligence on Earth and distributes karma.

Galactic Web: A large, planet-encircling grid created by the consciousness of all things on Earth—humans, animals, plants, and minerals. Magnetic Vortices, namely the Golden Cities, appear at certain intersections. The Ascended Masters often refer to different types of energy points (i.e. Chakra, lei-line, Golden City Vortex, etc.) in the Galactic Web. Since the Angelic Host protects this Web of Creation, the protective web of the Angelic Host is often synonymous with the Galactic Web.

Garden of Existence: The Garden of Eden.

Gobean: The first United States Golden City located in the states of Arizona and New Mexico. Its qualities are cooperation, harmony, and peace. Its Ray Force is blue, and its Master Teacher is El Morya.

Gobi: A Golden City named for the Great Desert of China, *Gobi* in Mongolian means "the waterless place." Ascended Masters claim the Golden City of Gobi is a step-down transformer for the energies of the Earth's first Golden City—Shamballa. Gobi's esoteric definition comes from the Chinese translation of "go—across," and *bi* in Indonesian (Abun, A Nden, and Yimbun dialects) means "star." The Golden City of Gobi means "Across the Star," or "Across the Freedom Star." "Freedom Star" is a reference to Earth in her enlightened state.) Gobi aligns energies to the first Golden City of the New Times: Gobean.

Golden Age: A peaceful time on Earth prophesied to occur after the Time of Change. It is also prophesied that during this age, human life spans are increased and sacred knowledge is revered. During this time, the societies, cultures, and the governments of Earth reflect spiritual enlightenment through worldwide cooperation, compassion, charity, and love. Ascended Master teachings often refer to the Golden Age as the Golden-Crystal Age and the Age of Grace.

Golden Age of Kali Yuga: According to the classic Puranic timing of the Yugas, Earth is in a Kali-Yuga period that started around the year 3102 BCE the year that Krishna allegedly left the Earth. During this time period, which according to this Puranic timing lasts a total of 432,000 years—the ten-thousand year Golden Age period, also known as the Golden Age of Kali Yuga, is not in full force. Instead, it is a sub-cycle of higher light frequencies within an overall larger phase of less light energy.

This Golden Age is prophesied to raise the energy of Earth as additional light from the Galactic Center streams to our planet. This type of light is a non-visible, quasar-type light that is said to expand life spans and memory function, and nourish human consciousness, especially spiritual development. There are many theories as to when this prescient light energy began to flow to our planet. Some say it started about a thousand years ago, and others claim it began at the end of the nineteenth century. No doubt its influence has changed life on Earth for the better, and according to the I AM America Teachings, its effect began to encourage and guide human spiritual evolution around the year 2000 CE.

The Spiritual Teachers say that living in Golden Cities can magnify Galactic Energies and at their height, the energies will light the Earth between 45 to 48 percent—nearly reaching the light energies of a full-spectrum Treta Yuga or Silver Age on Earth. The Spiritual Teachers state, "The Golden Age is the period of time where harmony and peace shall be sustained."

Golden City Vortex: A Golden City Vortex—based on the Ascended Masters' I AM America material—are prophesied areas of safety and spiritual energies during the Times of Changes. Covering an expanse of land and air space, these sacred energy sites span more than 400 kilometers (270 miles) in diameter, with a vertical height of 400 kilometers (250 miles). Golden City Vortices, more importantly, reach beyond terrestrial significance and into the ethereal realm. This system of safe harbors acts as a group or universal mind within our galaxy, connecting information seamlessly and instantly with other beings. Fifty-one Golden City Vortices are stationed throughout the world, and each carries a different meaning, a combination of Ray Forces, and a Divine Purpose. A Golden City Vortex works on the principles of electromagnetism and geology. Vortices tend to appear near fault lines, possibly serving as conduits of inner-earth movement to terra firma. Golden Cities are symbolized by a Maltese Cross, whose sacred geometry determine their doorways, lei-lines, adjutant points, and coalescing Star energies. Since their energies intensify experiences with both the Fourth and Fifth Dimensions, Golden City Vortices play a vital role with the Ascension Process.

Gold(en) Ray: The Ray of Brotherhood, Cooperation, and Peace. The Gold Ray produces the qualities of perception, honesty, confidence, courage, and responsibility. It is also associated with leadership, independence, authority, ministration, and justice. The Gold Ray is currently influencing the spiritual growth and evolution of the divine HU-man. It is also associated with karmic justice and will instigate many changes throughout our planet including Earth Changes and social and economic change.

Golden Thread Axis: Also known as the Vertical Power Current. The Golden Thread Axis is physically composed of the Medullar Shushumna, a life-giving nadi physically comprising one-third of the human kundalini system. Two vital currents intertwine around the Golden Thread Axis: the lunar Ida Current, and the solar Pingala Current. According to the Master Teachers, the flow of the Golden Thread Axis begins with the I AM Presence, enters the Crown Chakra, and descends through the spinal system. It descends beyond the Base Chakra and travels to the core of the Earth. Esoteric scholars often refer to the axis as the Rod of Power, and it is symbolized by two spheres connected by an elongated rod. Ascended Master students and chelas frequently draw upon the energy of the Earth, through the Golden Thread Axis, for healing and renewal by using meditation, visualization, and breath techniques.

Great Central Sun: The great sun of our galaxy, around which all of the galaxy's solar systems rotate. The Great Central Sun is also known as the Galactic Center, which is the origin of the Seven Rays of Light and Sound on Earth.

Great White Brotherhood (Lodge): A fraternity of ascended and unascended men and women who are dedicated to the universal uplifting of humanity. Its main objective includes the preservation of the lost spirit, and the teachings of the ancient religions and philosophies of the world. Its mission is to reawaken the dormant ethical and spiritual sparks among the masses. In addition to fulfilling spiritual aims, the Great White Lodge pledges to protect mankind against the systematic assaults—which inhibit self-knowledge and personal growth—on individual and group freedoms.

Green Ray: The Ray of Active Intelligence is associated with education, thoughtfulness, communication, organization, the intellect, science, objectivity, and discrimination. It is also adaptable, rational, healing, and awakened. The Green Ray is affiliated with the planet Mercury. In the I AM America teachings the Green Ray is served by the Archangel Raphael and Archeia Mother Mary; the Elohim of Truth, Vista—also known as Cyclopea, and Virginia; the Ascended Masters Hilarion, Lord Sananda, Lady Viseria, Soltec, and Lady Master Meta.

Guru: Teacher.

Hall of Wisdom: Earth's Third Light Body that correlates to the Mesosphere is known as *Eshano*, an etheric Hall of Wisdom. It is associated with the collective consciousness of humanity. It is also the middle layer of atmosphere surrounding the Earth, and this companion energetic light body holds the collective etheric template or pattern for life on Earth. This light body is constantly changing to meet evolutionary needs. Because this ethereal light body holds the Master plan for life on Earth, it is affiliated with divine intelligence and reflects the collective Mental Body of humanity. The Spiritual Teachers refer to this light body as *Eshano*, which means "to have knowledge of Creation and what gives shape to Creation, or knowledge of that which comes from Created forms."

Harmony of the Spheres: A superior form of music, founded on beauty and harmonious combination, heard by those who have developed the ears to hear—clairaudience. The Harmony of the Spheres is an esoteric term that refers to an exacting form of balance and synchronization often realized through the hidden geometric and mathematical perfection of all created forms. The movement of the heavenly bodies is said to be timed to such mathematical precision and perfection that the planets create a celestial music.

Heart Chakra: The location of this chakra is in the center of the chest and is known in Sanskrit as the Anahata. Its main aspect is Love and Relationships; our ability to feel compassion, forgiveness, and our own feeling of Divine Purpose.

Higher Self: Said to reside in the spiritual planes of consciousness, the Higher Self is energetically connected to each individual in the physical plane, and is free from the karmas of the Earth Plane and identification with the material world. Sometimes the Ascended Masters refer to the Higher Self as the I AM Presence, as the Higher Self often bridges vital energies of the I AM Presence. They are however, entirely different from one another. The Higher Self oversees the human development of choice, the development of conscience, and conscious self-correction. Prayers and decrees to the Higher Self act with great efficacy, liberating the I AM Presence from Third Dimensional restraints of time and space. The Higher Self separates the developing human from the lower self (the animal nature) and is sometimes referred to as the Holy Spirit.

HU-man: The integrated and spiritually evolved human; the God Man.

HUE or HU, the: In Tibetan dialects, the word *hue* or *hu* means breath; however, the HU is a sacred sound and when chanted or meditated upon is said to represent the entire spectrum of the Seven Rays. Because of this, the HU powerfully invokes the presence of the Violet Flame, which is the activity of the Violet Ray and its inherent ability to transform and transmit energies to the next octave. HU is also considered an ancient name for God, and it is sung for spiritual enlightenment.

I AM: The presence of God.

I AM Presence: The individualized presence of God.

I AM THAT I AM: A phrase from Hebrew that translates to, "I Will Be What I Will Be." "I AM" is also derived from the Sanskrit *Om* (pronounced: A-U-M), whose three letters signify the three aspects of God as beginning, duration, and dissolution—Brahma, Vishnu, and Shiva. The AUM syllable is known as the omkara and translates to "I AM Existence," the name for God. "Soham," is yet another mystical Sanskrit name for God, which means "It is I," or "He is I." In Vedic philosophy, it is claimed that when a child cries, "Who am I?" the universe replies, "Soham—you are the same as I AM." The I AM teachings also use the name "Soham" in place of "I AM."

Immortality: Everlasting and deathless. Spiritual immortality embraces the idea of the eternal, unending existence of the soul. Physical immortality includes the notion of the timeless, deathless, and birthless body.

Initiation: Admission, especially into secret, advanced spiritual knowledge.

Inner Marriage: A process achieved through the spiritual integration of the masculine and feminine aspects of self, uniting dualistic qualities into greater balance and harmony for expression of self-Mastery.

Instant-Thought-Manifestation: The clear and concise use of thought to Co-create desires. The Master Teachers often refer to this process as Manifest Destiny. Experiences with Instant-Thought-Manifestation are said to prepare our consciousness to enter into the ONE.

Intention: Acts, thoughts, or conceptions earnestly fixed on something, or steadfastly directed. Intentions often reflect the state of an individual's mind which directs their specific actions toward an object or goal.

Judgment: The act of forming negative assumptions and critical opinions, primarily of fellow human beings.

Kali Yuga: The Age of Iron, or Age of Quarrel, when Earth receives twenty-five percent or less galactic light from the Great Central Sun.

Karma: Laws of Cause and Effect.

Klehma: The fifth United States Golden City located primarily in the states of Colorado and Kansas. Its qualities are continuity, balance, and harmony; its Ray force is white; and its Master Teacher is Serapis Bey.

Kuan Yin: The Bodhisattva of Compassion and teacher of Saint Germain. She is associated with all the Rays and the principle of femininity.

Kundalini: In Sanskrit, *kundalini* literally means coiled, and represents the coiled energy located at the base of the spine, often established in the lower Base and Sacral Chakras. Kundalini Shatki (shatki means energy) is claimed to initiate spiritual development, wisdom, knowledge, and enlightenment.

Law of Attraction and Repulsion: Physically, like charges repel; unlike charges attract. Through the Spiritual Law of Allowing, like attracts like.

Law of Love: Perhaps every religion on Earth is founded upon the Law of Love, as the notion to "treat others as you would like to be treated." The Law of Love, however, from the Ascended Master tradition is simply understood as consciously living without fear, or inflicting fear on others. The Fourth of the Twelve Jurisdictions instructs Love is the Law of Allowing, Maintaining, and Sustainability. All of these precepts distinguish love from an emotion or feeling, and observe Love as action, will, or choice. The Ascended Masters affirm, "If you live love, you will create love." This premise is fundamental to understanding the esoteric underpinnings of the Law of Love. The Master Teachers declare that through practicing the Law of Love one experiences acceptance and understanding; tolerance, alongside detachment. Metaphysically, the Law of Love allows different and varied perceptions of ONE experience, situation, or circumstance to exist simultaneously. From this viewpoint the Law of Love is the practice of tolerance.

Law of Rhythm: Everything ebbs and flows; rises and falls. The swing of the pendulum is universal. The measure of the momentum to the right is equal to the swing of the left.

Light: "Love in action."

Lord Apollo: A God of healing, truth, music, and Prophecy. Apollo and Diana serve as the second of the twelve Suns from the lineage of the Alpha-Omega Guardian Suns. The great Apollo is revered as the ancestral father to Saint Germain's heritage of spiritual knowledge and teaching. Additionally, Apollo is a sponsor for the Twelve Jurisdictions.

Lord Macaw or Lord Meru: An Ascended Master of the Ruby and Gold Ray is also known as the great Sage of Ancient Mu. Lord Meru is a teacher of the ancient civilizations of the Earth and considered a spiritual historian of their mythological records. Lord Meru is also known as Lord Macaw—the parrot—a symbol of beauty, wisdom, and spiritual knowledge. Lord Macaw's dark skin is contrasted by a colorful headdress filled with parrot, trogon, and quetzal bird feathers, a symbol of Quetzalcoatl—the Christ Consciousness. In the New Times, Lord Meru is prophesied to steward the Golden City of Gobi.

Lords of Venus: A group of Ascended Masters who came to serve humanity. They once resided on the planet Venus.

Love: "Light in action."

Malton: The second United States Golden City located in the states of Illinois and Indiana. Its qualities are fruition and attainment; its Ray force is Ruby and Gold; and its Master Teacher is Kuthumi.

Mantra: Certain sounds, syllables, and sets of words are deemed sacred and often carry the power to transmute karma, purify the spirit, and transform an individual. These are known as mantras. The mantra is a foundation of Vedic tradition and often treated as a devotional upaye—a remedial measure of difficult obstacles. Mantras, however, are not limited to Hinduism. Buddhists, Sikhs, and Jains also utilize mantras. The Ascended Masters occasionally provide mantras to chelas to improve resonance with certain Golden Cities.

Master Teacher: A spiritual teacher from a specific lineage of teachers—gurus. The teacher transmits and emits the energy from that collective lineage.

Mastery: Possessing the consummate skill of command and self-realization over thought, feeling, and action.

Meditation: Quieting or silencing the mind in order to give focused attention or devotion to one thing.

Mental Body: A subtle light body of the Human Aura comprising thoughts.

Monad: From an Ascended Master viewpoint, the Monad is the spark or flame of life of spiritual consciousness and it is also the Awakened Flame that is growing, evolving, and ultimately on the path to Ascension. Because of its presence of self-awareness and purpose, the Monad represents our dynamic will and the individualized presence of the Divine Father. Ultimately, the Monad is the spark of consciousness that is self-determining, spiritually awake, and drives the growth of human consciousness. The Monad is the indivisible, whole, divine life center of an evolving soul that is immortal and contains the momentum within itself to drive consciousness to learn, grow, and perfect itself in its evolutionary journey.

New Day: The process of seeing or perceiving a problem or an obstacle from a different point of view. This often involves a shift in consciousness.

ONE: Indivisible, whole, harmonious Unity.

Oneness: A combination of two or more, which creates the whole.

Oneship: A combination of many, which comprises the whole and, when divided, contains both feminine and masculine characteristics.

Oral Tradition: According to the Master Teachers and many indigenous teachers, the Oral Tradition, or learning through oral instruction, is the preferred medium to receive spiritual knowledge. This method requires the use of memory and memorization and also instigates the recognition of vital, yet subtle nuances that engender spiritual comprehension and may include the Master Teacher's use of telepathy, clairaudience, and clairvoyance.

Perception: Awareness through the senses, including the super-senses.

Pink Flame: Energy of Divine Love that is held in the consciousness of most Bodhisattvas, primarily Kuan Yin. It is alleged to surround the human heart.

Pink Ray: The Pink Ray is the energy of the Divine Mother and associated with the Moon. It is affiliated with these qualities: loving, nurturing, hopeful, heartfelt, compassionate, considerate, communicative, intuitive, friendly, humane, tolerant, adoring.

Point of Perception: A Co-creation teaching of the Ascended Masters and its processes pivot on the fulcrum of choice. By carefully choosing certain actions, a Master of Choice opens the world of possibility through honing carefully cultivated perceptions, attitudes, beliefs, thoughts, and feelings. This allows the development of outcome through various scenarios and opens the multi-dimensional door to multiple realities and simultaneous experiences that dissolve linear timeframes into the Ever Present Now.

Prana: Vital, life-sustaining energy; also known as orgone or chi.

Prophecies of Change: Primarily prophecies of Earth Changes, but also include political, social, and cultural change alongside spiritual and biological changes to humanity.

Prophecies of Peace: Prophecies and spiritual teachings aimed toward humanity's spiritual growth, evolution, and entrance into the New Times and the Golden Age.

Prophecy: A spiritual teaching given simultaneously with a warning. It's designed to change, alter, lessen, or mitigate the prophesied warning. This caveat may be literal or metaphoric; the outcome of these events are contingent on the choices and the consciousness of those willing to apply the teachings.

Purification: A clearing process, especially in spiritual practice, which frees consciousness from encumbering or objectionable elements.

Quetzalcoatl: The Quetzalcoatl Energies, as explained and taught by Lord Meru, are akin to the Christ energies when applied in the esoteric Western Christian tradition. Quetzalcoatl, the deity, was an ancient spiritual teacher, predating Christ and his teachings likely had roots in alchemic Atlantean (Toltec) teaching. Quetzalcoatl, in contemporary terms, is the Incan Christ.

Rapture: A form of spiritual liberation, based on sincerity, peace, faith, and acceptance.

Ray: A force containing a purpose, which divides its efforts into two measurable and perceptible powers: light and sound.

Ruby Ray: The Ruby Ray is the energy of the Divine Masculine and Spiritual Warrior. It is associated with these qualities: energetic; passionate; devoted; determination; dutiful; dependable; direct; insightful; inventive; technical; skilled; forceful. This Ray Force is astrologically affiliated with the planet Mars and the Archangel Uriel, Lord Sananda, and Master Kuthumi. The Ruby Ray is often paired with the Gold Ray, which symbolizes Divine Father. The Ruby Ray is the evolutionary Ray Force of both the base and solar chakras of the HU-man; and the Gold and Ruby Rays step-down and radiate sublime energies into six Golden Cities.

Sacred Geometry: Esoteric scholars suggest that diverse universal patterns, geometrical shapes, and geometric proportions symbolize spiritual balance and perfection.

Saint Germain: Ascended Master of the Seventh Ray, Saint Germain is known for his work with the Violet Flame of Mercy, Transmutation, Alchemy, and Forgiveness. He is the sponsor of the Americas and the I AM America material. Many other teachers and Masters affiliated with the Great White Brotherhood assist his endeavors.

Sananda: The name used by Master Jesus in his ascended state of consciousness. Sananda means joy and bliss, and his teachings focus on revealing the savior and heavenly kingdom within.

Serapis Bey: An Ascended Master from Venus who works on the White Ray. He is the great disciplinarian—essential for Ascension—and works closely with all unascended humanity who remain focused for its attainment.

Seven Rays: The traditional Seven Rays of Light and Sound are: the Blue Ray of Truth; the Yellow Ray of Wisdom; the Pink Ray of Love; the White Ray of Purity; the Green Ray of Healing; the Gold and Ruby Ray of Ministration; and the Violet Ray of Transmutation.

Seventh Manu: Highly evolved lifestreams that embody on Earth between 1981 to 3650. Their goal is to anchor freedom and the qualities of the Seventh Ray to the conscious activity on this planet. They are prophesied as the generation of peace and grace for the Golden Age. South America is their forecasted home, though small groups will incarnate in other areas of the globe.

Shalahah: The fourth United States Golden City located primarily in the states of Montana and Idaho. Its qualities are abundance, prosperity, and healing; its Ray Force is Green; and its Master Teacher is Sananda.

Shamballa: Venusian volunteers, who arrived 900 years before their leader Sanat Kumara, built the Earth's first Golden City. Known as the City of White, located in the present-day Gobi Desert, its purpose was to hold conscious light for the Earth and to sustain her evolutionary place in the solar system.

Shroud of Darkness: Inhibiting beliefs that obscure the soul's direct contact with their innate Conscious Immortality.

Simultaneous Reality: A nonlinear perspective of time. It prepares us for potential possibilities in all situations—past, present, and future—and retains the capacity for multiple encounters and outcomes. Each reality exists side by side, so humans can consciously open up to these events to gain insight and self-knowledge.

Solar Plexus: Also known as the Navel Chakra, this chakra is located between the navel and the base of the sternum. It is an intense feeling (intuitive) chakra which is known as the Center of Power and Balance in relationship to everything in life.

Spiritual Awakening: Conscious awareness of personal experiences and existence beyond the physical, material world. Consequently, an internalization of one's true nature and relationship to life is revealed, freeing one of the lesser self (ego) and engendering contact with the higher (Christ) self and the I AM.

Spiritual Liberation: The process whereby the soul gains freedom from the Wheel of Karma, and the need to reincarnate in a physical body on Earth. In Ascended Master Teachings, spiritual liberation is known as Ascension. Depending on the spiritual level and evolution of each soul, after spiritual liberation from the Earth Plane the soul travels onward into higher levels of Astral or Causal Planes, where yet another liberation process ensues. This new level of consciousness and spiritual evolution may include Earth or other planets. In Hinduism, spiritual liberation is known as moksha, which is the release from suffering and the cycle of death and rebirth. It is claimed that the soul is released from duality as the concept of self expands into the sublime realization of the I AM and the soul merges with the I AM Presence. This also includes the realization of the Christ Consciousness or birth of the Quetzalcoatl energies as the soul enters Fourth and Fifth Dimensional Awareness. This perfected state of consciousness realizes the Earthly Plane as illusion or Maya and exists without separation from the God Source, the spiritually free at-one-ment.

Spiritual Preparedness: The practice and application of various spiritual techniques and disciplines that help to increase and leverage spiritual potential alongside the Ascension Process during the Time of Change.

Star (of a Golden City): The apex, or center of each Golden City.

Star Seed: Souls and groups whose genetic origins are not from Earth. Many remain linked to one another from one lifetime to the next, as signified by the Atma Karaka, a Sanskrit term meaning "soul indicator." Star-seed consciousness is often referred to by the Spiritual Teachers as a family or soul group whose members have evolved to and share Fifth-Dimensional awareness. Star Seeds can also contain members who have not yet evolved to this level, who are still incarnating on Earth.

Step-down Transformer: The processes instigated through the Cellular Awakening rapidly advance human light bodies. Synchronized with an Ascended Master's will, the awakened cells of light and love evolve the skills of a Step-Down Transformer to efficiently transmit and distribute currents of Ascended Master energy—referred to as an Ascended Master Current (A.M. Current). This metaphysical form of intentional inductive coupling creates an ethereal power grid that can be used for all types of healing.

Third Dimension: Thought, feeling, and action.

Third Eye: Also known as the Ajna Chakra. This energy center is located above and between the eyebrows. The Third-eye Chakra blends thought and feeling into perception and projection for Co-creative activity.

Thousand Eyes: This term refers to the endless rounds of death and rebirth the soul encounters before entering the Ascension Process of spiritual liberation.

Time Compaction: An anomaly produced as we enter into the prophesied Time of Change. Our perception of time compresses; time seems to speed by. The unfolding of events accelerates, and situations are jammed into a short period of time. This experience of time will become more prevalent as we get closer to the period of cataclysmic Earth Changes.

Time of Change: The period of time currently underway. Tremendous changes in our society, cultures, and politics in tandem with individual and collective spiritual awakenings and transformations will abound. These events occur simultaneously with the possibilities of massive global warming, climactic changes, and seismic and volcanic activity—Earth Changes. The Time of Change guides Earth to a new time, the Golden Age.

Time of Testing: The Time of Testing is a period of seven to twenty years which began around the turn of the twenty-first century, following the time period known as the Time of Transition. According to Saint Germain and other Ascended Masters, the Time of Testing is perhaps one of the most turbulent periods mankind will experience and its first seven years is prophesied as a period of change and strife for many. As its title suggests, the Master Teachers claim this timeframe may challenge students by testing their spiritual acumen and inner strength.

Transportation Vortex: Prophesied to develop as we enter the New Times, a model of this energy anomaly will exist in the Golden City of Shalahah near Coeur d'Alene, Idaho (USA). This interdimensional portal functions through the developed projection of the mind. As our understanding of Ray Forces evolves, our bodies take on a finer quality in light and substance and we are able to bilocate through these energy Vortices. In the New Times this becomes an accepted form of travel.

True Memory: Memory, as defined by Ascended Master teachings, is not seen as a function of the brain, or the soul's recall of past events. Instead, True Memory is achieved through cultivating our perceptions and adjusting our individual perspective of a situation to the multiple juxtapositions of opinion and experience. This depth of understanding gives clarity and illumination to every experience. Our skill and Mastery through True Memory moves our consciousness beyond common experiences to individualized experiences whose perceptive power hones honesty and accountability. The innate truth obtained from many experiences through the interplay of multiple roles creates True Memory, and opens the detached and unconditional Law of Love to the chela.

Twelve Jurisdictions: Twelve laws (virtues) for the New Times that guide consciousness to Co-create the Golden Age. They are Harmony, Abundance, Clarity, Love, Service, Illumination, Cooperation, Charity, Desire, Faith, Stillness, Creation/Creativity.

Twin Flame: The idea that the ONE creative spark of the soul's genesis divides into two distinct parts: one part female, the other part male. The twin aspects of the soul play a number of roles with each other throughout successive lifetimes, and as the soul evolves and spiritually grows, this interaction perfects and expands.

Unana: Unity Consciousness.

Unfed Flame: The three-fold flame of divinity that exists in the heart and becomes larger as it evolves. The three flames represent Love (pink); Wisdom (yellow); and Power (blue).

Vertical Power Current: See Golden Thread Axis.

Violet Flame: The Violet Flame is the practice of balancing karmas of the past through Transmutation, Forgiveness, and Mercy. The result is an opening of the Spiritual Heart and the development of bhakti—unconditional love and compassion. It came into existence when the Lords of Venus first transmitted the Violet Flame, also knows as Violet Fire, at the end of Lemuria to clear the Earth's etheric and psychic realms, and the lower physical atmosphere of negative forces and energies. This paved the way for the Atlanteans, who used it during religious ceremonies and as a visible marker of temples. The Violet Flame also induces Alchemy. Violet light emits the shortest wavelength and the highest frequency in the spectrum, so it induces a point of transition to the next octave of light.

Violet Flame Angels: Legions of Violet Flame Angels are claimed to carry the energies of the transmuting Violet Flame whenever they are called upon. The Angels of the Violet Flame protect the flame in its purity and dispense its transforming vibration.

Wahanee: The third United States Golden City located primarily in the states of South Carolina and Georgia. Its qualities are justice, liberty, and freedom; its Ray Force is violet; and its Master Teacher is Saint Germain.

White Ray: The Ray of the Divine Feminine is primarily associated with the planet Venus. It is affiliated with beauty, balance, purity, and cooperation. In the I AM America teachings the White Ray is served by the Archangel Gabriel and Archeia Hope; the Elohim Astrea and Claire; and the Ascended Masters Serapis Bey, Paul the Devoted, Reya, the Lady Masters Venus and Se Ray, and the Group of Twelve.

Will: Choice.

Write and Burn Technique: An esoteric technique venerated by Ascended Master students and chelas to transmute any unwanted situation or circumstance, primarily dysfunctional life patterns. This technique involves handwriting and then burning a letter—a petition—to the I AM Presence for Healing and Divine Intervention.

Appendix A

The Gold Ray

The Ascended Masters Kuthumi and Saint Germain both prophesy that the Gold Ray is the most important energy force currently present on Earth. While its presence catalyzes the spiritual growth of the HU-man, it is also associated with Karmic Justice and will instigate change at all levels: Earth Changes, economic and social change.

The Master Teachers prophesy that its appearance fosters the dawn of a New Consciousness for humanity, which ends the turbulence of Kali Yuga and ushers in a 10,000-year time of spiritual potential and opportunity for all—the Golden Age of Kali Yuga.

Saint Germain gives this decree to initiate the stream of the New Consciousness within:

> Mighty Golden Ray, stream forth now,
> into the heart of the consciousness of
> humanity.
> Mighty Golden Ray, bring forth new
> understanding.
> Bring forth a new Spiritual Awakening.
> Bring forth complete and total divinity
> In the name of I AM THAT I AM.
> So be it.

This decree allows the Brotherhood to give further aid and contact to individuals who desire the Masters' help and assistance for spiritual development.

The Gold Ray initiates and transforms through the spiritual principles of balance and harmony. Working through the Hermetic Principle of vibration, Saint Germain claims that the Gold Ray creates, "Absolute Harmony." This sublime Ray of Consciousness also helps the chela to shape and form the will and align our emotions and inevitably our actions to the Divine Will. It enters into the Seventh Chakra and its current flows alongside the Golden Thread Axis (Medullar Shushumna). The ideal of Unana—the ONE—is initiated and inevitably created through the presence of the Gold Ray. Saint Germain suggests this decree for the Violet Flame to prepare spiritual consciousness to receive and apply the influence of the Gold Ray.

Mighty Violet Ray,
Come forth in all transmuting action.
Mighty Violet Ray,
Come forth now and dissolve all discord
and the cause and effect of all that is
holding me
from understanding and moving forward
into the new Golden Age.
I call this forth in the name of
That mighty Christ I AM.
So be it.

The Gold Ray assists humanity's evolution at this important time. This process is calibrated by the premise of vibration and is a developmental step associated with the use of the Violet Flame. Those who apply this teaching may notice a golden tinge in their light bodies, hear a high-pitch sound, or celestial music (the Harmony of the Spheres) before falling asleep or upon awakening. As the Gold Ray floods the Earth with energies to evolve human consciousness this energy is controlled by both the Galactic Center and further calibrated by the Spiritual Hierarchy for humanity.

Appendix B

The Lightfields of Ascension:

First Light Body: The *Electronic Blueprint* holds the electrical impulse in the light body; therefore, it is similar to the *Auric Blueprint*. It is charged with the energy of the Seven Major Chakras, the energy grids, meridians, and nadis. It resembles a grid, and is blue in color. This layer of the Human Aura contains a distinctive pulse that is synchronized with the individual's heartbeat, and lies within several inches of the physical body.

Second Light Body: The *Emotional Field* holds our instincts, feelings, and emotions. This light body is normally a vibrant pink in color. It is associated with the magnetism of the physical body. This light body is most affected by sound, especially mantras and decrees. Because varied emotions can change the characteristics of this light body, the light body can fluctuate in color. Extreme anger or violence can turn the light body dark red, while spiritual feelings of devotion can alter it to a visible light pink with hues of green. This light body is observed four to six inches from the physical body.

Third Light Body: The *Mental Body* carries our distinct thoughts, ideas, and perceptions. This energy field, to some degree, is associated with intelligence and our capability to process and implement information. This light body is associated with the color yellow, although some individuals display mental bodies that are vibrant gold. It is located six inches to one foot from the physical body.

First Three Light Bodies: The first three light bodies represent Action (electronic blueprint), Feeling (emotion) and Thought (mental). These three primary colors also represent the Unfed Flame of Power, Love, and Wisdom, respectively. The first three light bodies of the Human Aura endure throughout the Earthly incarnation, and dissipate with the death of the physical body.

Fourth Light Body: The fourth light body of the human is the *Astral Body*. This is the energy body that we use when we dream and travel at night, via different meditation techniques. It is varied in color, but often displays a rainbow of pastel colors: blues, pinks, greens, and purples. It is located a foot, to a foot and a half, from the physical body. Advanced souls often display a larger Astral Body of luminous white light, with iridescent pastels. This light body, along with the next three higher light bodies, survives the death of the physical body, and then resides in the Astral Plane for further spiritual development to prepare for the next incarnation.

Fifth Light Body: This body of energy is known as the *Auric Template*, and is similar to the Electronic Template. However, this field of vital energy gives form according to individual states of consciousness. It radiates approximately one and a half to two feet from the physical body. It is the energy layer from where a seasoned energy practitioner can detect and treat disease. The color of this energy body can vary depending on the individual strength of Ray Forces.

Sixth Light Body: This energy body carries the individual's aspirations and beliefs. Many refer to this energy body as the *Celestial Body*, but it is also known as the *Spiritual Emotional Body*. This body is often connected to feelings of bliss, unconditional love, and interconnectedness. It can be reached through meditation. This layer extends two to nearly three feet from the physical body. It is colored with opalescent pastels. Some energy practitioners report a gold-silver light shining throughout this energy body. Master Teachers, Spirit Guides, and Spiritual Teachers often enter this energy field to communicate with an individual, or to revive and heal the physical body. The Sixth and Seventh Light Bodies hold varying levels of the Akashic Records.

Seventh Light Body: The *Causal Body* is the last of the human energy bodies. It is an egg-shape ovoid that holds all of the lower energy bodies in place with extremely strong threads of light that form a golden grid. This energy body is also known as the *Spiritual Mental Body*, and contains the *Golden Thread Axis*, also known as the *Tube of Light* that connects one to the I AM Presence. Energy practitioners allege that this energy body holds the Akashic records that are keys to past-life memory. This energy body extends approximately three feet around the body but can be larger, depending on the spiritual evolution of the individual.

As human spiritual evolution advances, we begin to develop new energy bodies of light, sound, and experience. The Spiritual Teachers mention that the HU-man, the developed God Man, can acquire eight new distinct energy bodies beyond the initial, primary Seven Light Bodies. The Fifteenth Energy Body propels the soul out of duality, free from both physical and astral restraint.

An Ascended Master contains and influences twenty-two light bodies. Apparently, Light Bodies Eight through Ten have the ability to contend with varying light spectrums beyond Third Dimension and can manage space-time, including time contraction, time dilation, and time compaction. But more importantly, the development of the HU-man Energy system implements the ever-important Ascension Process. The following information shares descriptions of the HU-man Energy Bodies Eight, Nine, and Ten.

Eighth Light Body: Known as the *Buddha Body* or the *Field of Awakening*, this energy body is initially three to four feet from the human body. It begins by developing two visible grid-like spheres of light that form in the front and in the back of the Human Aura. The front sphere is located three to four feet in front of and between the Heart and Solar Plexus Chakras. The back sphere is located in front of and between the Will-to-Love and Solar Will Chakras. These spheres activate an ovoid of light that surrounds the entire human body; an energy field associated with harmonizing and perfecting the Ascension Process. This is the first step toward Mastery. Once developed and sustained, this energy body grants physical longevity and is associated with immortality. It is known as the first level of Co-creation, and is developed through control of the diet and disciplined breath techniques. Once this light body reaches full development, the spheres dissipate and dissolve into a refined energy field, resembling a metallic armor. The mature Eighth Light Body then contracts and condenses, to reside within several inches of the physical body where it emits a silver-blue sheen.

Ninth Light Body: This body of light is known as *The Divine Blueprint*, as it represents the innate perfection of the divine HU-man. It is an energy field that is developed through uniting dual forces, and requires an in-depth purification of thought. In fact, this energy field causes the soul to face and Master those negative, dark, forces that the Spiritual Teachers refer to as a type of *mental purgatory*. This energy body processes extreme fears and transmutes them. The transmutation completely restructures beliefs, and purifies energies held in the lower mental bodies accumulated throughout all lifetimes. This produces an alchemizing, divine, HU-man Mental Body that develops approximately thirty-six feet from the human body.

This energy field first appears as nine independent triangular-gridded spheres. Apparently, the nine glowing spheres grow in circumference and, inevitably, morph into one glowing energy body. As the Ninth Light Body develops, it is extremely responsive to telepathy and group thought, and progresses to act and influence collective thought and consciousness. In its early to mid-stages of development, this energy body emits a high frequency violet light that evolves into the alchemic Violet Flame. The Spiritual Teachers claim that the decree, "I AM the Presence of Collective Thought," is its energetic mantra. The refined energies of the mature Divine Blueprint inevitably contract and concentrate in a similar manner to the Eighth Light Body. As it draws its auric field closer to the physical body; within two to four inches, it radiates gold and then a bluish-silver light that reflects the strength of its protective shield.

Tenth Light Body: This is the final level of three protective HU-man light bodies, which is formed through the purification of desires, and is known as the *Diamond Mind*. Because this energy body gathers thought as light, it is a substantive and sizeable light body. The Spiritual Teachers often refer to the three protective HU-man energy bodies as the *Triple Gems*, and together they are strong enough to pierce human illusion. Combined with the four higher primal energy bodies—the Fourth Light Body to the Seventh Light Body—the total sum of these energy bodies produces the alchemic number seven. In this septagonal order, the Diamond Mind helps to produce the *Lighted Stance* and the inevitable attainment of the *Seamless Garment.*

The Lighted Stance is a state of conscious perfection—a precursor to Ascension. The soul's ability to manifest the Seamless Garment bestows the Master with the ability to travel and experience the Astral and Physical planes without spiritual corruption or physical disintegration. This mature energy body compacts itself to reside approximately six inches from the physical body, and is alleged to have the strength and brilliance of "ten-thousand diamonds." This energy body also exhibits complete Mastery over thought, feeling, and action—the first three primal human Energy Bodies, and can dissolve or manifest their physical presence at will; or, it can take form for whatever cause, circumstance, or "task at hand," without any limitation.

Appendix C

The Eight-sided Cell of Perfection through the Dimensions:

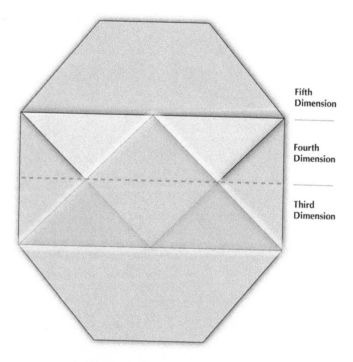

Fifth
Dimension

Fourth
Dimension

Third
Dimension

The Third, Fourth, and Fifth Dimensions
within the Eight-Sided Cell of Perfection.

Appendix D

Location of the Eight-sided Cell of Perfection:

FIGURE 9-A
*Eight-Sided Cell of Perfection
within the Heart*
(Left) According to the Ascended Masters, the Eight-Sided Cell of Perfection is an atomic cell located within the human heart. The cell holds the Unfed Flame, which matures and grows with spiritual development and evolution. The Eight-Sided Cell carries each individual's divinity.[1]

---

1. *Häggström, Mikael. "File:Human Heart.png." Wikimedia Commons. 13 Apr. 2010. Web. 27 Jan. 2011.*

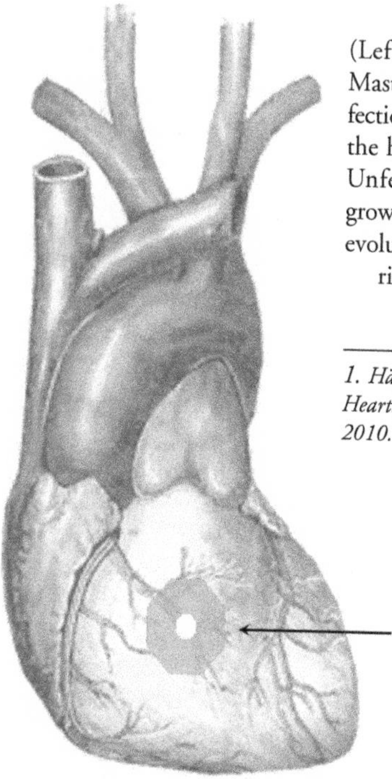

The Eight-sided Cell
of Perfection holds the
Flame within the Heart
(not to scale)

Appendix E

The Twilight Breath of Luminous Light:

The Twilight Luminous Light Breath is best practiced during early sunrise to cultivate masculine energy, and in the soft sunset colors of pinks and blues to cultivate feminine energy. Focus upon the Third Eye and inhale and exhale through the nose. Visualize your breath moving into your Heart Chakra. This expands energy to the heart center and into the Eight-sided Cell of Perfection. As you become more experienced with this process, the stream of breath becomes cool and calming as it moves from the Third Eye, and onto its expansion in the heart.

If you'd like to speed this process, place a cool cloth or an ice cube on your Third Eye as you inhale the first breath. Your energy pathways will immediately sense the chill. Then visualize the cool energy moving into your heart center. As you continue your daily practice, eventually discard the cool cloth or ice. You will begin to notice the cool temperature of the breath without the use of a cloth or ice moving through your energy pathways.

Saint Germain recommends lighting a physical fire as a celebration of the Violet Flame before practicing the breath. After the fire is lit, sit near its flames as you practice the Twilight Breath technique. This ceremonial fire is equivalent to a *puja*—a fire ceremony that helps one to shed physical karmas and accelerate the process of spiritual liberation. Plus, fire is cleansing to the chakra system. Leonard Orr writes about fire and its ability to help clear our lightfields and achieve physical immortality, "When we sit or sleep near an open flame, the wheels of our energy body (our aura) turn through the flames and are cleaned. The emotional pollution of participating in the world is burned away. Death urges are dissolved by fire and water together as they clean and balance the energy body. Fire is as important as food. Fire may be the highest element of God and requires the most intelligence to use. It is perhaps the most neglected natural divine element of God in our civilization."[1]

The Twilight Breath activates the divine Eight-sided Cell of Perfection that resides in conjunction with the Mighty I AM Presence. The I AM Presence connects to the ONE, Unana, and the I AM that I AM.

---

1. Orr, Leonard. *"Breaking the Death Habit." Rivendell Village, 2 May 2008.*

Appendix F

The Violet Flame:

Simply stated, the Violet Flame stabilizes past karmas through Transmutation, Forgiveness, and Mercy. This leads to the opening of the spiritual heart and the development of bhakti—the unconditional love and compassion for others. Our Co-creative ability is activated through the Ascended Master's gift of the Unfed Flame in adjunct with the practice of the Law of Love, and the Power of Intention. But the Violet Flame, capable of engendering our greatest spiritual growth and evolution, is spiritual velocity pure and simple.

Invoking the flame's force often produces feelings of peace, tranquility, and inner harmony—its ability to lift the low-vibrating energy fields of blame, despair, and fear into forgiveness and understanding, paves the path to love.

The history of the Violet Flame reaches back thousands of years before the Time of Christ. According to Ascended Master legend, the Lords of Venus transmitted the Violet Flame as a spiritual consciousness during the final days of the pre-Atlantis civilization Lemuria. As one society perished and another bloomed, the power of the Violet Flame shifted, opening the way for Atlantean religiosity. This transfer of power initiated a clearing of the Earth's etheric and psychic realms, and purged the lower physical atmosphere of negative forces and energies. Recorded narratives of Atlantis claim that Seven Temples of Purification sat atop visible materializations of the Violet Flame. The archangels Zadkiel and Amethyst, representing freedom, forgiveness and joy, presided over an Atlantean Brotherhood known as the Order of Zadkiel, also associated with Saint Germain. These Violet Flame Temples still exist today in the celestial realm over Cuba.

The Violet Flame benefits humans and divinities equally. During spiritual visualizations, meditations, prayers, decrees, and mantras, many disciples seek the Violet Flame for serenity and wisdom. Meanwhile, the Ascended Masters always use it in inner retreats—even Saint Germain taps into its power to perfect and apply its force with chelas and students

The Violet Flame, rooted in Alchemic powers, is sometimes identified as a higher energy of Saturn and the Blue Ray, a force leavened with justice, love, and wisdom. Ascended-Master lore explains the Violet Flame's ability to release a person from temporal concerns: Saturn's detachment from emotions and low-lying energies sever worldly connections. That's why the scientific properties of violet light are so important in metaphysical terms. The shortness of its wavelength and the high vibration of its frequency induce a point of transition to the next octave of light and into a keener consciousness.

Appendix G

Golden Cities through the Dimensions:

Golden Cities Through the Dimensions	THIRD DIMENSION	FOURTH DIMENSION	FIFTH DIMENSION
EVOLUTIONARY ARCHETYPE	The awakened, conscious human.	The HU-man Nature Beings	Ascended Masters Elohim Archangels Evolutionary Archetypes
COMMUNITY	Golden City Community. Harmonious connection to Mother Earth. Stewardship	Elemental Kingdom Mineral Kingdom Plant Kingdom Animal Kingdoms Nature Kingdoms	Shamballa (Spiritually perfected community.)
ACTIVITY	Longevity Slower aging process. Greater healing and recovery ability. Physical Regeneration (Cell replication)	Telepathic Ability Psychic Ability Development of the Super Senses. Lucid Dreaming Multi-dimensional awareness.	Unana Consciousness of the ONE. Fellowship through the ONE and Oneship.
PLANE	Physical	Astral	Causal
TIME	Duality Linear Time Continuous time is a series of transactions.	Time Compaction Time Warp Deja Vue Peak or Zone Experience	Timelessness The Abiding Presence Ever Present Now Continuous Flow
SOCIAL	Human Rights Civil Rights Twelve Jurisdictions	Group Mind Collective Consciousness Brotherhood and Sisterhood	Unity
CULTURE	Cultivation of the Four Pillars: Arts, Languages, Sciences, Ancient Religions and History, Philosophy	Beauty, Harmony, Cooperation	Grace Peace

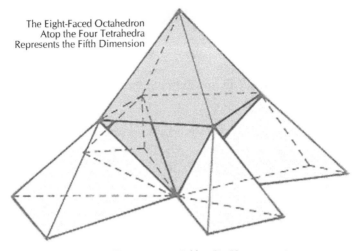

The Eight-Faced Octahedron
Atop the Four Tetrahedra
Represents the Fifth Dimension

Fifth Dimension: Golden City Vortex
The Fifth Dimension is represented by a Octahedron in the Golden City Structure

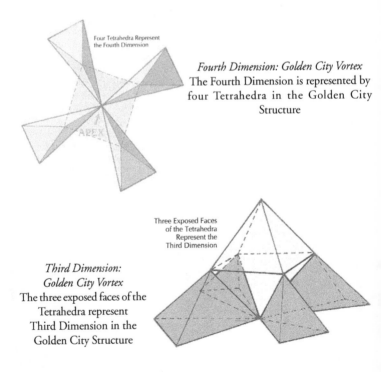

Four Tetrahedra Represent
the Fourth Dimension

APEX

Fourth Dimension: Golden City Vortex
The Fourth Dimension is represented by
four Tetrahedra in the Golden City
Structure

Three Exposed Faces
of the Tetrahedra
Represent the
Third Dimension

Third Dimension:
Golden City Vortex
The three exposed faces of the
Tetrahedra represent
Third Dimension in the
Golden City Structure

Appendix H

Golden Ray Diet:

The Golden Ray diet is a supplemental regime that you can add to your everyday meals to increase the Gold Ray throughout your energy system. It consists of fruits, vegetables, legumes, and grains whose plants, rinds, pods, or skins turn an orange or yellow color upon maturation. The plant must grow above the ground, no root vegetables. The plant absorbs the Gold Ray from our Sun. Here are a few suggestions:

Fruits:
Orange
Lemon
Banana
Grapefruit
Tangerine
Peach
Gold Kiwi
Yellow Dragonfruit
Yellow Raspberry
Mango
Pineapple
Yellow Apple
Yellow Fig
Yellow Pear
Nectarine
Persimmon
Papaya

Vegetables:
Sweet Yellow Pepper
Yellow Squash
Pumpkin
Yellow Cauliflower
Yellow Wax Bean

Nuts:
Cashew
Almonds (ripe)

Beans and Grains:
Garbanzo Bean
Yellow Lentil
Yellow Split Pea
Quinoa
Wheat
Barley
Oats

Appendix I

Saint Germain on Economics and Nations:
On occassion Saint Germain prophesies the worldwide economic return to gold and silver standards. This also includes the elimination of fiat currencies and establishment of true state economies. His teachings also recommend democratic republics and open societies. A brief definition of these terms follows.

True State Economy:
A time will come when the world's economy implodes and paper money becomes obsolete, even prohibited. Only then will a new economic paradigm emerge—one that relies on the trading of precious metals, natural resources, and tangible goods. The nascent economy, resembling a Natural Economy, is based on what it produces. This structure eliminates the need to transfer goods, resources, and services via traditional currency.

Republic:
A republic, in simple terms, is a political body led by an elected official, such as a president or consul, rather than a sovereign leader. It follows some type of charter (e.g. the Constitution), which directs the government to elect representatives who will advance national interests and support the right of self-determination. Though the terms republic and democracy, a system where majority rules, are often used synonymously, the general idea of these political philosophies differ in principle. A republic, in theory, serves the common good of its citizens whom are subject to the Rule of Law. America in its current state is a republic—consider the Pledge of Allegiance: "I pledge allegiance to the Flag of the United States of America, and to the Republic, for which it stands ..."

Open Society:

Developed by philosopher Henri Bergson, an open society supports the human rights and the political freedoms of its citizens. In theory, an open society is just that: open. The government avoids keeping secrets from the public; rather, it places emphasis on tolerance, transparency, flexibility, and personal responsibility. In his book, *The Open Society and Its Enemies,* Austrian-born illuminato Sir Karl Popper defined an open society as one that allows its populace to throw out the leaders peacefully and without bloodshed. Compare this notion to a closed society—an unpredictable supremacy defined by violent revolutions and riotous coups d'etat.

Appendix J

The Unfed Flame and Sacred Iconography:

In Buddhism the Unfed Flame is depicted as the *Triple Gem*, or the *Three Refuges*. The Triple Gem is reflected in the Third Dimension as the Unfed Flame held in the physical heart. In the Fifth Dimension, the Triple Gem embodies three important processes for humanity's spiritual unfoldment:

1. Recognition of the innate Divinity that exists within all.
2. Practice of the spiritual teachings that lead to liberation—Dharma.
3. Active membership among the community of those who have attained enlightenment and liberation: the Great White Brotherhood.

The Triple Gem

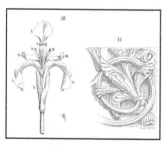

The Fleur-de-lis

Buddhists attribute the spiritual consciousness of the Triple Gem to the creation of the, "diamond mind which can cut through illusion."[1] The esoteric symbol of the resurrection of the spirit through the stillness of Ascension is the *Fleur-de-lis* which is a symbol of royalty and literally means *lily flower*.[2] Like the Triple Gem of the Buddhists, some Ascended Master teachings compare the Fleur-de-lis to the Unfed Flame.

---

1. Wikipedia, *Three Jewels*, http://en.wikipedia.org/wiki/Three_Jewels, (2011).
2. Ibid.

Appendix K

The Fourfold Flame:

A graphic representation of the Fourfold Flame within the Eight-sided Cell of Perfection. The Unfed Flame originates through the three vital flames of Love, Wisdom, and Power. The fourth flame is the flame of desire—*of the source.* The fourth flame empowers our Divine Co-creativity ability and the consciousness of Unana, or unity.

Appendix L

Levels of Mastery through the Eight-sided Cell of Perfection:

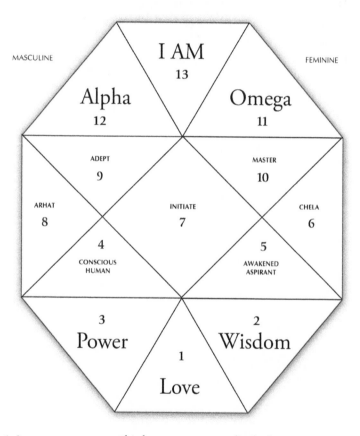

1. Love	Third	Individualization
2. Wisdom	Third	Individualization
3. Power	Third	Individualization
4. Conscious Human	Third and Fourth	Conscience
5. Awakened Aspirant	Third and Fourth	Spiritual Awakening

6. Chela	Third, Fourth, and Fifth	Spiritual Discipline
7. Initiate	Third, Fourth, and Fifth	Spiritual Experience
8. Arhat	Third, Fourth, and Fifth	Spiritual Control, Buddha Consciousness
9. Adept	Fourth and Fifth	Spiritual Mastery
10. Master	Fourth and Fifth	Spiritual Liberation
11. Omega	Fourth and Fifth	Christ Consciousness
12. Alpha	Fourth and Fifth	Ascension
13. I AM	Fourth and Fifth	Ascended Master: I AM THAT I AM

Appendix M

The Seventh Manu and the Swaddling Cloth:

The Master Teachers describe the Seventh Manu as a large group of souls that incarnate for over 1,500 years on Earth (1981 AD to 3650 AD). The purpose of the Seventh Manu soul-group is to raise the overall vibration of Earth through their spiritually evolved understanding of Freedom and Peace. Their attributes include:

1. Many of the souls incarnating as the wave of souls known as the Seventh Manu have not incarnated on Earth for thousands of years; and some were last present on Earth during the time of Atlantis.

2. Some souls of the Seventh Manu have a natural talent and propensity toward the technological sciences, which inevitably assists the Earth and its evolutionary process.

3. Previous incarnations on diverse planets and different solar systems are common among Seventh Manu souls. According to Saint Germain, the system of evolving souls does not consider physical proximities restricted only to Earth. The soul is "timeless" and is not bound by the Third Dimensional aspects of time and space. When viewed through this understanding, the veil separating physical and spiritual realities is a thin line of demarcation, and the soul's consciousness often evolves between galaxies and star-systems literally thousands of light-years away.

4. The New Children are prophesied as spiritual Masters who will incarnate on Earth at a critical juncture of humanity's evolutionary process to help the masses transmute difficult Karmas and lead many into the liberation, or Ascension Process.

5. Children of the Seventh Manu are also known as the *Indigo Children*. Seventh Manu refers to the Seventh Alchemic Ray—the Violet Ray. The scientific wavelength of the color Indigo is between Blue and Violet; however, many consider Indigo analogous to Purple.

6. Since Seventh Manu souls carry a higher vibration and less Karmic burden than the average Earth soul, they are prophesied to lead humanity into the *Age of Transportation*. During this Earth epoch, spiritual technology will embrace the ancient practice of bi-location and the spiritual ideals of timelessness.

7. The Spiritual Technology of the children of the Seventh Manu is prophesied to develop and is derived from varied experiences gleaned from their incarnations in different galaxies. This exposes the Earth to new ideas, processes, and perceptions that evolve our current sciences and reshape much of our current technology.

8. The influence of the New Manu children will shape human consciousness for several thousand years. As these souls are wise beyond their years, they will be seen as the new elders of Earth. The New Children will lead a renaissance in reformation of our societies, cultures, religions, and scientific knowledge.

9. While this group of souls is highly evolved, Saint Germain explains that they, too, have their own unique Karmas and "Time of Testing," to be played out upon the Earth Plane and Planet.

*The Swaddling Cloth
of South America*

The Swaddling Cloth is the homeland for the Seventh Manu, a group of souls prophesied to incarnate during the New Times.

From: *Freedom Star World Map*, I AM America Seventh Ray Publishing

The Swaddling Cloth

An area of over a million square miles located in Brazil, South America. According to the Ascended Masters, this area is the primary prophesied physical location for the incarnation of the children of the Seventh Manu. The Swaddling Cloth is protected by the Ascended Master Mother Mary. *See above map.*

Appendix N

The Cellular Awakening:

This spiritual initiation, activated by Master Teachers Saint Germain and Kuthumi, prepares the consciousness to recognize and receive instruction from the Fourth Dimension. Cellular Awakening stimulates seven subtle adjustments on the cellular level, preparing the physical body for an intense spiritual experience. These acclimatizations include:

- **The Quickening:** An acceleration of cells throughout the body creating a union with the I AM Presence.
- **Higher Metabolism:** This physical change activates the Eight-Sided Cell of Perfection, which is located in the heart. According to the Master Teachers, a person can inspire this phenomenon by fasting for twenty-four hours on citrus juices containing a portion of orange, lemon, tangerine, and grapefruit.
- **Attunement to the Galactic Beam:** Also known as the Eighth or Golden Ray, this process prepares the physical body to receive the beneficial results of the Violet Flame. The Galactic Beam emits a high-frequency energy. The Earth receives this power from the Great Central Sun. According to the Master Teachers, frequent saltwater baths with two cups of salt and three to four drops atomidine (iodine supplement) will augment this process. [Atomidine is available from the Heritage Store: www.heritagestore.com]
- **Violet Flame:** This powerful universal force disintegrates etheric genetic coding through daily meditation, visualization, and decrees. Saint Germain says that kindling the Violet Flame during the Cellular Awakening affects the water balance of the physical body, including circulation, the lymphatic system, and the emotional body.
- **Diet:** During Cellular Awakening the Master Teachers say to avoid or reduce all animal products from the diet.

Appendix O

Archetypal Knowledge:

The spiritual knowledge and teachings of the Ascended Masters are often based upon archetypes. This form of universal spiritual knowledge quickly enters the human psychology, and deeply affects spiritual growth and evolution. Swiss psychiatrist Carl Jung identified five basic archetypes that comprise the human mental framework: [1]

1. The Self (Individualization)
2. The Shadow (the Dark Side)
3. Anima (Feminine image held by the masculine.)
4. Animus (Masculine image held by the feminine.)
5. Persona (the Masked Self)

The works of William Shakespeare are renowned for the use of archetypes, and the Tarot is perhaps one of the best-known esoteric versions of universal myth. Archetypes weave in, through, and around the art of storytelling, and the Ascended Masters apply their exacting simplicity for humanity's spiritual growth and transformation. Here are some of the underlying archetypes of the teachers of Ascended Master lore:

- El Morya: The strong, silent type; Divine Father.
- Saint Germain: The Magician; Divine Brother.
- Soltec: The Scientist.
- Hilarion: The Physician and Healer.
- Sanat Kumara and Lord Macaw: The Sage.
- Lady Portia: The Wise Woman; Divine Sister.
- Kuthumi: The Agrarian and nature-lover; the Ecologist.

---

1. *"Jungian Archetypes." Wikipedia. Accessed August 19, 2016. https:// en.wikipedia.org/wiki/Jungian_archetypes.*

- Mother Mary: The Western feminine archetype; Divine Mother.
- Kuan Yin: The Eastern feminine archetype; Divine Mother.
- Sananda and Lord Macaw: The realized Christ/Quetzalcoatl; Divine Masculine; Divine Son.
- Mary Magdalene: Divine Feminine; Divine Daughter.
- Lady Nada: Feminine archetype of justice, strength, and equality; Divine Sister.
- Lady Master Venus: Feminine archetype of beauty and harmony; Divine Feminine.

Appendix P

Devas and the Elemental Kingdom:

Deva, meaning *shining one* or *being of light*, is a Sanskrit word that describes a God, deity, or spirit. Helena Blavatsky, co-founder of the Theosophical Society, introduced these celestial beings, or angels, to the Western World in the nineteenth century. She described them as progressed entities from previous incarnations that would remain dormant until humanity attained a higher level of spiritual consciousness. Devas represent moral values and work directly with nature kingdoms.[1]

Elementals, on the other hand, are an invisible, subhuman group of creatures that act as counterparts to visible nature on terra firma. Medieval alchemist and occultist Paracelsus coined the term for these Elemental spirits. He divided them into the following four categories: gnomes (earth); undines (water); sylphs (air); and salamanders (fire).

- **Gnomes:** The term comes from the Greek word "genomus" or "Earth dweller." These subterranean spirits work closely with the Earth, giving them immense power over rocks, flora, gemstones, and precious minerals; they are often guardians of hidden treasures. Some gnomes gather in families while others remain indigenous to the substances they serve or guard. Members of this group include elves, brownies, dryads, and the little people of the woods.[2]
- **Undines:** These fairylike pixies, the deification of femininity, synchronize with the earth element, water. Their

1. Orin Bridges, *Photographing Beings of Light: Images of Nature and Beyond* (Highland City, FL: Rainbow Press, Inc.), page 57.
2. Manly Hall, *The Secret Teachings of All Ages, Diamond Jubilee Edition* (Los Angeles: Philosophical Research Society, Inc.), pages 106-107.

essence is so closely tied to aquatic milieus that they possess the power to control the course and function of water. Undines, imbued with extraordinary beauty, symmetry, and grace, inhabit riparian environments—rivers, streams, lakes, waterfalls, and swamps. According to mythical lore, these lithe spirits, also known as naiads, water sprites, sea maids, and mermaids, assume male or female identities. Sioux legend says water deities, or wak'teexi in the native tongue, often incarnate as human beings: a telltale blue birthmark on the body will bare their original identities.[3]

- **Sylphs:** The most evolved of the four Elementals, sylphs—often synonymous with fairies and cherubs—are beautiful, lively, diaphanous, yet mortal demigods. They represent the vaporous element of air and the expression of the female essence. Omnipresent, sylphs float in the clouds and in the ether, though their true home lies in mountaintop hamlets. There, they erect sacred sanctuaries for the Gods. This spritely covey, blessed with millennium-passing longevity and highly developed senses of sight, hearing, and smell, are particularly receptive to the voices of the Gods—that's why theosophical scholars believe the ancients used sylphs as oracles. Guided by Paralda, the king of air, and a communal of female sylphs known as sylphides, sylphs occasionally assume a petite human form. They are intelligent, mutable, and loyal to humans.[4]

- **Salamanders:** Salamanders represent the invisible Elemental spirit of fire and the embodiment of the male divinity; without their existence, warmth wouldn't exist. Working through the blood stream, body temperature, and the liver, salamanders produce heat in humans and animals. Some theosophical scholars say this class of El-

3. Richard Dieterle, *Waterspirits (Wak'teexi)* (http://www.hotcakencyclopedia.com/ho.Waterspirits.html), (2005).

4. Manly Hall, *The Secret Teachings of All Ages, Diamond Jubilee Edition* (Los Angeles: Philosophical Research Society, Inc.), pages 107-108.

ementals occupies balmy Southern regions. The mystical salamander encompasses much more than its amphibious counterparts. According to esoteric teachings, these fabled creatures manifest distinctly different forms. At approximately twelve inches in length, the lizard like salamander is physically tantamount to its terrestrial Urodela cousin. But, unlike earthly species, ethereal salamanders thrive in fire and slither through flames. Lore describes another group of salamanders as a race of giant creatures that wear flowing robes, don protective armor, and emit a fiery, incandescent glow. According to Medieval tradition, the third coterie of these entities are descendents of the great salamander Oromasis—son of the enigmatic Greek, Zarathustra. But the Acthnici, ruled by the Elemental king Djinn, are the most powerful and feared faction of salamanders. They travel as indistinct globes of light, especially over water. Voyagers and sailors often experience Acthnici at sea as glowing forks of flame on the masts and the riggings of ships. They call this phenomenon St. Elmo's Fire. Scholars and other savants encourage others to avoid these salamanders. The price of knowing them, they say, outweigh the benefits.[5]

5. Manly Hall, *The Secret Teachings of All Ages, Diamond Jubilee Edition* (Los Angeles: Philosophical Research Society, Inc.), pages 107-108.

Appendix Q

Lineage of Gurus:
The importance of the lineage of the gurus who sponsor a specific spiritual practice cannot be underestimated. This detailed history is in essence the ancestry of the technique, and those who perfected its nuance, potency, and innate perfection. Moreover, when using a meditation, decree, or mantra suggested by a Master Teacher you are psychically tugging on its ancestral root and the sum total of energy of those who previously taught and mastered the methods. This is why it is often recommended in certain decrees and prayers to call upon a specific lineage of teachers and Masters. By doing so invokes their remarkable presence and timely assistance.

Throughout the *I AM America Teachings*, Saint Germain and others have shared insights on the lineage of not only spiritual practices, but the lineage of Christ Consciousness, Shamballa, specific Golden Cities, and hierarchal offices. Examples of these remarkable pedigrees of renowned gurus, Masters, founders of world religions, and spiritual archetypes follow.

Lineage of the Violet Flame:
Saint Germain → Kuan Yin → the Elohim Arcturus and Diana

Lineage of the Christ Consciousness:
Kuthumi, El Morya, Saint Germain → Sananda → Lord Maitreya → Lord Meru → Quetzalcoatl → Lord Apollo

Lineage of the Gold Ray:
Kuthumi → Lord Lanto → Helios, Vesta, and Lord Apollo → Alpha and Omega → Elohae and Eloha

Lineage of the Twelve Jurisdictions:
Saint Germain → Sananda → Lady Master Venus, Sanat Kumara as the Cosmic Christ (Kartikkeya, Kumar, Skanda, Guha) → Lord Apollo

Golden City Lineage:
Remaining 49 Golden Cities → Golden City of Gobean → Golden City of Gobi → Shamballa → City of the Kumaras (Venus)

Golden City Hierarch Lineage:
El Morya → Lord Meru → Lord Maitreya → Sanat Kumara → Lords of Venus

Shamballa Creation Lineage:
Serapis Bey → Lord Gautama, Lord Maitreya, and the Lords of the Flame → Sanat Kumara → the Three Kumaras → Lords of Venus

Golden City of Gobean Lineage:
El Morya → Serapis Bey → Akhenaton → Quetzalcoatl

Lord of the World (Shamballa) :
Sananda (as Lord of the Transition) → The Buddha (Lord Lanto) → World Teacher (will be Saint Germain, currently Lord Maitreya) → Lord of the World (now Gautama Buddha, formerly held by Sanat Kumara who was preceded by Sri Maga)

World Teacher:
Saint Germain → Sananda → Lord Maitreya

Saint Germain's Lineage of Gurus:
Saint Germain → Sananda → Lady Portia, Lord Maitreya → Kuan Yin → Lord Apollo

Lineage of the Galactic Suns:
Osiris and Isis, Apollo and Diana, Krishna and Sophia, Helios and Vesta (Earth's Sun), Hercules and Amazonia, Aureole and Aurea, Dawn and Luz → Alpha and Omega → Elohae and Eloha

Lineage for the Seventh Manu (the New Children):
Goddess Yemanya (the Second Sister) and Pachamama (the Third Sister) → Goddess Meru (the first Sister) → Mother Mary

Appendix R

Adjutant Points of a Golden City:

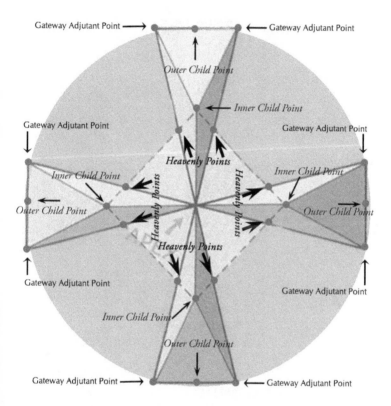

A Golden City possesses seventeen Adjutant Points that comprise the Christ Consciousness. (Gateway Points, Child Points, plus the Star). The Eight Heavenly Points comprise the Eight-sided Cell of Perfection.

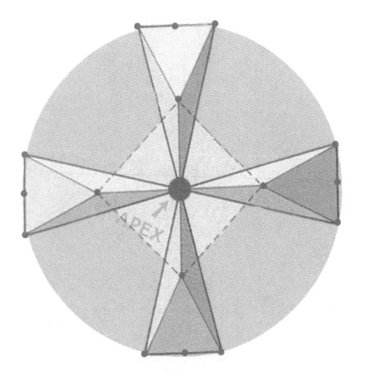

The seventeen vital Adjutant Points of a Golden City
that comprise the Christ Consciousness. These Adjutant
Points represent both Third and Fourth Dimension.

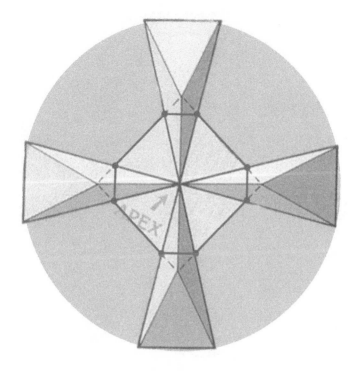

The Eight-sided Cell of Perfection is created by the eight
Heavenly Adjutant Points. These Adjutant Points represent
both Fourth and Fifth Dimesnion.

Appendix S

Spiritual Pilgrimage and Migratory Pathways:

Migratory pathways are spiritual pilgrimages that travel through a specific series of Adjutant Points to create a specific energy, vibration, or frequency within the light bodies. Spiritual migrations function through the Ascended Master spiritual precepts of sacrifice, and energy for energy. Golden City pilgrimages are often intense, and filled with adventure, new insights, and spiritual awakening. There are many different patterns for different desired results. For instance, when first traveling to Golden Cities it is suggested to enter first through the Eastern Door, travel onward to the Southern Door, then to the Western Door, and conclude in the Northern Door. Visits to Adjutant Points in this pilgramage are not necessary. This is an opportunity to acclimate your energies to Fourth and Fifth Dimensional experience, the residing Hierarch of the Golden City, and the Golden City's magnificent Ray Force.

The classic migratory pathway to initiate a chela to the mysteries of the Adjutant Points is a pilgrimage through all of the four doorways and the primary Adjutant Points. The chela travels through a series of seventeen Adjutant Points, total. This migratory pathway begins in the Northern Door West Adjutant Point, travels onward to the Northern Door East Adjutant Point, then to the Northern Door Outer Child Adjutant Point, and then to the Northern Door Inner Child Adjutant Point. This four-point pilgrimage concludes the Northern Door.

This spiritual pilgrimage continues through the East Door and starts in the Eastern Door North Adjutant Point, then to the Eastern Door South Adjutant Point, travels next to the Eastern Door Outer Child Point, and concludes in the Eastern Door Inner Child Point.

The spiritual pilgrimage continues onward to the Southern Door and starts in the Southern Door East Adjutant Point, moves to the Southern Door West Adjutant Point, the third stop is the Southern Door Outer Child Adjutant Point, and concludes in the Southern Door Inner Child Point. Again, this four-point pilgrimage completes the migration through the Southern Door.

The Western Door migration begins at the Western Door Southern Adjutant Point, moves next to the Western Door Northern Adjutant Point, the third migration is to the Western Door Outer Child Point, and onward to the Western Door Inner Child Adjutant Point. This concludes the migratory pathway in the Western Door.

The final point is the Golden City's Star. There the spiritual pilgrimage ends with prayer, ceremony, and meditation in the sublime energies of the Star—where the spiritual light of the four doorways coalesce. This seventeenth point symbolizes the birth of the Christ Consciousness within, integration with the I AM Presence, and the Ascension.

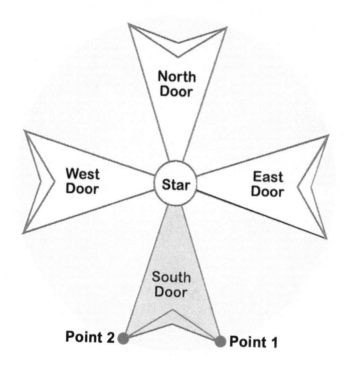

Evolutionary Body Migration

The Evolutionary Body Migration pattern starts in the Southern Door, at its Eastern point. Then travel west to the next point in the Southern Door.

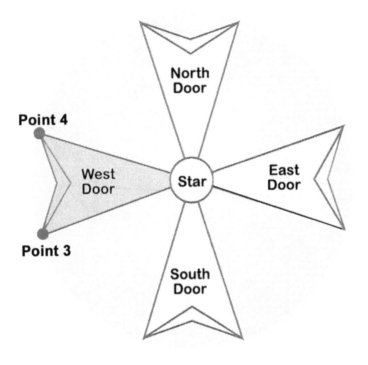

Proceed to the Western Door and its southerly point. You will travel onward to the northerly point of the Western Door.

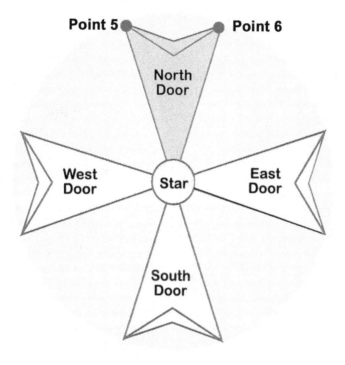

The westerly point of the Northern Door is your next stop. Then travel east, to the Northern door's next point as diagrammed.

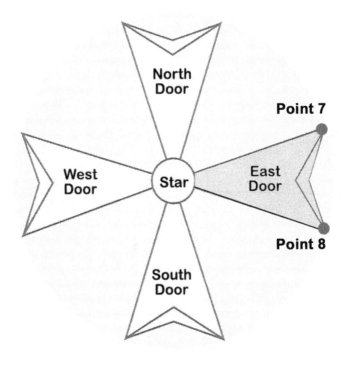

Your migration continues to the northerly point of the Eastern Door. Then travel onward to the southern point of the Eastern Door.

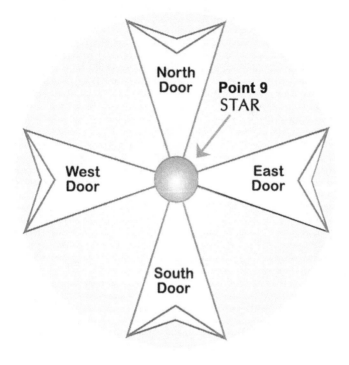

The *Evolutionary Body Migration* concludes in the Star, where you can offer your prayers and decrees, and practice meditation with your personal Spirit Guides and the residing Master Teacher of the Golden City Vortex.

Appendix T

Master Kuthumi and Lady Nada:
In the late nineteenth century, Ascended Master Kuthumi—also known as Koot Hoomi or K. H.—collaborated with Helena Blavatsky and El Morya to introduce humanity to the spiritual teachings of theosophy. And like Master M., K. H. is dedicated to advancing the spiritual fitness of mankind to a higher consciousness. Thus, Kuthumi approached his interaction with humans in the same manner as his mahatma contemporary: he veiled his identity behind the Indian dignitaries of the time, in this case, Thakar Singh Sandhawalia, leader of the Singh Sabha movement. Founded in the early 1870s, this Indian independence campaign emerged as a grassroots effort to maintain the purity of Sikhism, otherwise eroded by Christian Missionaries. Sandhanwalia, Ranbir Singh—one of El Morya's aliases—and H. P. B. joined forces to spread theosophy throughout India.

Kuthumi and El Morya shared a close relationship through the ages. Both trained by the Ascended Master Maha Chohan, the spiritual duo, as two of the wise men, paid homage to the baby Jesus: K. H. as Balthazar and Master M. as Melchior. Kuthumi also shows up as Sir Percival at the round table of King Arthur (aka El Morya). But his incarnation history isn't limited to associations with his spiritual Brother. Kuthumi's past lifetimes include the Greek philosopher Pythagoras; Thutmose III, the warrior pharaoh of the eighteenth dynasty; Shah Jahan, the emperor of India and builder of the Taj Mahal; and founder of the Franciscans, Saint Francis of Assisi. Highly educated and extremely private, Kuthumi, a Cambridge University alumni, spent 200 years in seclusion in the Himalayan Mountains before ascending in 1889. He is a gentle Master affiliated with the Golden City Malton, and the Gold and Ruby Rays of ministration and service to humanity. In one of his earliest letters to A. P. Sinnett, Kuthumi calls the holy Golden Temple of the Sikhs his home, although he's seldom there, preferring the solitude of Tibet.[3]

Author Alice Bailey, who continued to work with the Masters after Blavatsky's death in 1891, writes about a visit from K. H.: "Master Koot Hoomi, [is] a Master who is very close to the Christ." In 1895, Kuthumi told the fifteen-year-old Bailey that she would travel the world "doing your Master's work all the time" and that "I would have to give up being such an unpleasant little girl and must try and get some measure of self-control. My future usefulness to him and to the world was dependent upon how I handled myself and the changes I could manage to make."[1]

A. D. K. Luk writes of Kuthumi: "He was such a lover of nature that he would watch a certain phase for hours, or would stay a whole day with a flower to see it open into full bloom, and perhaps watch it close again at night. He was one of the few who represented the heart of the Nature Kingdom. He was able to read through the Elemental Kingdom and accelerate his consciousness to a point where he was of assistance in that realm. Birds and animals were drawn to him to be in his radiance which was about him; drawn by his constant attention and adoration to his Source."[2]

Lady Nada is the Ascended Goddess of Justice and Peace who is associated with Mastery of speech (vibration), communication, interpretation, and the sacred Word. Nada is also known as a divine advocate of Universal Law, and she is often symbolized by the scales of blind justice.

Esoteric researchers document Lady Nada's historical narrative of the last days of Atlantis, including the archetypal building of an Ark by Noah, a Master Guru to many ancient Atlanteans. As a member of his mystery school, she escaped the demise of the iconic continent of marbled temples and geomantically engineered streets to an established retreat of the Archangels. Bands of ships sailed to the

1. Bailey, Alice A., *Unfinished Autobiography* (New York: Lucis Publishing Company), page 36.
2. Luk, A. D. K., *Law of Life, Book II* (Pueblo, CO: ADK Luk Publications), page 275.

higher grounds of North and South America, Europe, and the Himalayas. Upon arrival to the mountainous sanctuary she was personally tutored by the Archangel Charity.

The youngest of a large Atlantean refugee family, Nada was an extraordinarily gifted child. At Archangel Charity's sublime temple, she focused upon meditation and the expansion of the Unfed Flame within her Eight-sided Cell of Perfection. After she achieved her ascension, she commented about her final lifetime, "I saw the victory of each of my brothers and sisters, the fullness of my joy was in a heart of love expanded . . . but I took my leave into the higher octaves, thoroughly understanding the meaning of self-mastery and the pink flame."[3]

Lady Nada is primarily known for her service on the Pink Ray, however she is presently associated with the Yellow Ray of Wisdom, and the Ruby and Gold Rays of Ministration, Brotherhood, and Service. She lovingly serves with Master Kuthumi to assist the Deva and Elemental Kingdoms in the Golden City of Malton (Illinois and Indiana, USA) and the Golden City of Denasha (Scotland).

Lady Nada is the tender yet steadfast hierarch of the Scottish highland's Denasha, and Master Kuthumi is the much beloved hierarch of Malton—a Golden City filled with forests, lakes, and benevolent nature spirits.

---

3. Prophet, *The Masters and Their Retreats* (Corwin Springs, MT: Summit University Press), pages 274-275.

Appendix U

The Science of Twilight:

Sunrise is the point where the Sun is ascending to the horizon and sunset is the point where the Sun is descending from the horizon. There are three perceptions of twilight, depending on your observational point. These three systems are used for different forms of science and navigation.

1. **Civil** uses a terrestrial point that establishes a clear line of vision of the horizon and is measured at six degrees below the horizon. Light is visible and you can see landforms in the defused light.

2. **Nautical** is viewed upon the water and requires clear weather and a calm sea to establish a line of vision. The Sun measurement is twelve degrees below the horizon. Light is more diffused than civil, but the water enhances the luminosity across the horizon.

3. **Astronomical** is eighteen degrees below the horizon. The light is most diffused and can be a mixture of moonlight and other stars.

Appendix V

The Golden Age of Kali Yuga

As early as 1988, the Master Teachers often referred to the "Time of Transition"—a twelve-year period where humanity would experience tremendous growth in spirituality and knowledge that transforms personally and globally. This period was replaced in the year 2000 with the "Time of Testing," a seven- to twenty-year period where economies and societies would encounter instability and insecurities. These years will also mark a period of spiritual growth for humanity where brotherly love and compassion will play a key role in the development of Earth's civilizations as we globally move toward "The Age of Cooperation." During the Age of Cooperation, which is prophesied to last several thousand years, humanity will mark another New Age. The Master Teachers prophesy that these times will be recorded in history as one of Earth's Golden Ages.

Interestingly, other time systems concur with this Prophecy. Even though we are experiencing a darker time on Earth due to the influence of Kali Yuga (Kali Yuga's total reign lasts 432,000 years), some Vedic scholars see a glimmer of hope for humanity in the 10,000-year period known as the Golden Age within Kali Yuga. And we are experiencing this now.

Apparently, Kali Yuga began approximately 5,000 years ago. But according to the Bhavishya Purana, global changes and tribulations began around the year 2000 AD, alongside a continuous upswing in spiritual consciousness due to the influence of the Golden Age of Kali Yuga, which some say began around the year 1500 AD, others calculate that it began around 1898 AD. (The Bhavishya Purana is said to be one of the oldest and reliable Vedic scriptures on prediction; it accurately predicted the coming of Jesus,

Muhammad, and Buddha.) This lesser cycle of light within a greater cycle of darkness will only last for 10,000 years and then the full effects of Kali Yuga (sans the Golden Age) will ensue. The Golden Age that we are now experiencing is considered to be a very important time for humanity's spiritual growth and evolution. Stephen Knapp, author of *The Vedic Prophecies*, writes, "During the period within the golden age of Kali Yuga, the spiritual opportunity for people increases, although we can plainly see that the standards for moral and spiritual principles also continue to decrease at the same time amongst most people, but not quite as rapidly. So it is a time that all people should try to take advantage of, because once it's over, you haven't seen anything yet." Clearly, this bright spot in an overall dismal cycle is given to "make hay, while the sun is shining."

Since the light of the central Sun, or Galactic Center, regulates the intelligence of humanity during the cycles of the Yugas, some Vedic authorities argue that mathematical calculations made during the darkness of Kali are inaccurate. This is the theory of Sri Yuteswar, disciple of Avatar Babaji and Paramahansa Yogananda's Master Teacher. He writes in *The Holy Science*, "The mistake crept into the almanac for the first time about 700 BC, during the reign of Parikshit, just after completion of the last Descending Dwapara Yuga ... Together with all the wise men of his court, (he) retired to the Himalayan Mountains, the paradise of the world. Thus there were none in the court of Raja Parikshit who could understand the principle of correctly calculating the ages of the several Yugas." (It has been suggested that once the Rishis fled for refuge to the Himalayas, that they also took the sacred knowledge of Vastu Shastra—the Vedic science of Earth's geomancy—which later evolved into Chinese Feng Shui.)

The following table reflects the timing of the Yugas, based on the work of Sri Yuteswar. Using this approach, in the year 2000 we have already experienced 300 years of a Bronze Age—Dwapara Yuga in the cycle of Ascension. It is also important to note that the Yuteswar Yuga Cycle (often referred to as the "Electric Cycle") is based on the movement of light through declining and ascending cycles. This descending cycle ceases at the lowest point and then begins an upward motion in the ascending cycle to the highest point of light. From a practical point of view, this would seem to make more sense than the commonly held viewpoint, prophesying a Golden Age directly following an age of Iron. This method reflects a more natural progression of light—i.e., spring, summer, fall, and winter, not winter directly to summer.

DESCENDING LIGHT	AGES	ASCENDING LIGHT
11,501 BC to 6701 BC	GOLDEN *(Krita)*	7699 AD to 12,499 AD
6701 BC to 3101 BC	SILVER *(Treta)*	4099 AD to 7699 AD
3101 BC to 701 BC	BRONZE *(Dwapara)*	1699 AD to 4099 AD
701 BC to 499 BC	IRON *(Kali)*	499 AD to 1699 AD

It is also important to understand that the Yuteswar Cycle uses a shorter cycle with just 24,000 years in one complete cycle. The traditional cycle contains 432,000 years, which begins in the year 3102 BC. So, which one is correct? Optimistically, the shorter cycle is a much more pleasant viewpoint, marking an obvious upward trend for humanity's growth and evolution. But it is entirely possible that we are experiencing two trends simultaneously—an overall downward phase containing a smaller, minor upward cycle as taught by Sri Yuteswar. Dr. David Frawley, Vedic authority and teacher of the ancient wisdom, addresses the issue: "I see humanity to be in a greater dark age phase, because even in the Golden and Silver Ages of the lesser cycle as evidenced in the Vedas, the great majority of human beings appear to remain on a materialistic or vital plane level, concerned mainly with the ordinary goals of family, wealth, and personal happiness. Only the higher portion of humanity, the cultural elite of a few percent, appears to experience the full benefits of the ages of light. This is the same as today, when the majority of human beings live on the same emotional level as before, and only a few really understand the secrets of science and technology, though all benefit from them."

If you overlay both systems, we are definitely experiencing an upward trend, major or minor, with the cycle of descending light beginning in the years 11,500 AD to 12,499 AD. Often the Master Teachers remind us, "The minutes and seconds tick . . . the Awakening is at hand. The time has come for man to receive the gift!" No doubt, we are living in an important time. And it is a time where we can begin, with the assistance of the upward cycle of Galactic Light, to evolve and develop through a finer harmonic. So why wait? "The time is now."

Appendix W

Ascended Masters of the I AM America Teachings
Saint Germain, the Holy Brother:
The Lord of the Seventh Ray and the Master of the Violet
Flame, Saint Germain lived numerous noteworthy lifetimes,
dating back thousands of years, before incarnating as the
Comte de Saint Germain during Renaissance Europe. He lived
as the Englishman Sir Francis Bacon, the sixteenth-century
philosopher, essayist, and Utopian who greatly influenced
the philosophy of inductive science. His most profound and
well-known work on the restoration of humanity, the Instau-
ratio Magna (Great Restoration), defined him as an icon of
the Elizabethan era. Research also shows his co-authoring of
many Shakespearean sonnets.

According to Esoteric historians, Queen Elizabeth I of Eng-
land—The Virgin Queen—was his biological mother. Before
Bacon's birth, the queen married Earl of Leicester, quieting
ideas of illegitimacy. Elizabeth's lady in waiting, Lady Ann
Bacon, wife of the Lord High Chancellor of England, adopted
him following the stillbirth of her baby. Bacon was, therefore, the true heir to the crown and England's rightful king.[1]
But his cousin James I of Scotland succeeded the throne.
Sir Bacon described this turn of events in his book, Novum
Organo, published in 1620: "It is an immense ocean that surrounds the island of Truth." And Saint Germain often re-
minds us to this day "there are no mistakes, ever, ever, ever."

Bacon's philosophies also helped define the principles of
Free Masonry and democracy. As an adept leader of the Rosi-
crucians (a secret society of that time), he set out to reveal
the obsolescence and oppression of European monarchies.

---

1. Marie Bauer Hall, *Foundations Unearthed,* originally issued as *Francis Bacon's*
Great Virginia Vault, Fourth Edition (Los Angeles: Veritas Press), page 9.

Eventually, Bacon's destiny morphed. He shed his physical form and sought the greatest gift of all: immortality. And that's what placed him in the most extraordinary circumstances throughout history. Even his death (or lack of) evokes controversy. Some say Bacon faked his demise in 1626—the coffin contained the carcass of a dog.

According to the author, ADK Luk, Saint Germain ascended on May 1, 1684 in Transylvania at the Rakoczy mansion. He was 123 years old. Some say Saint Germain spent the lost years—from 1626 to 1684—in Tibet. During this time he took (or may have been given) the name Kajaeshra. Interpreted as God's helper of life and wisdom, it was possibly a secret name and rarely used. Kaja has several interpretations: in Greek it means pure; Balinese, toward the mountain; early Latin (Estonian), echo; Hopi, wise child; Polish, of the Gods; and Hebrew, life. The second part of the name—Eshra (Ezra)—translates into help or aid.

Indeed, Bacon's work would impact centuries to follow. During his time in Tibet, tucked away in silent monasteries, Germain designed a society that eventually created a United Brotherhood of the Earth: Solomon's Temple of the Future. It's a metaphor used to describe the raising of consciousness as the greater work of democracy. Author Marie Bauer Hall studied the life of Francis Bacon. In her book, Foundations Unearthed, she described the legendary edifice: "This great temple was to be supported by the four mighty pillars of history, science, philosophy, and religion, which were to bear the lofty dome of Universal Fellowship and Peace."[2]

But Germain embraced an even deeper passion: the people and nation of America, christening it New Atlantis. He envisioned this land—present-day United States, Canada, Mexico, and South America—as part of the United Democracies of Europe and the People of the World. America, this growing society, held his hope for a future guided by a Democratic Brotherhood.

---

2. Marie Bauer Hall, *Foundations Unearthed,* originally issued as *Francis Bacon's Great Virginia Vault,* Fourth Edition (Los Angeles: Veritas Press), page 13.

The Comte de Saint Germain emerged years later in the courts of pre-revolutionary France—his appearance, intelligence, and worldliness baffled members of the Court of Versailles. This gentleman carried the essence of eternal youth: he was a skilled artist and musician; he spoke fluent German, English, French, Italian, Portuguese, Spanish, Greek, Latin, Sanskrit, Arabic, and Chinese; and he was a proficient chemist. Meanwhile, literary, philosophic, and political aristocracy of the time sought his company. French philosophers Jean-Jacque Rousseau and Voltaire; the Italian adventurer Giacomo Casanova; and the Earl of Chatham and statesman Sir Robert Walpole of Britain were among his friends.

In courts throughout Europe, he dazzled royalty with his Mastery of Alchemy, removing flaws from gems and turning lead into Gold. And the extent of Germain's ken reached well into the theosophical realm. A guru of yogic and tantric disciplines, he possessed highly developed telepathic and psychic abilities. This preternatural knowledge led to the development of a cartographic Prophecy—the Map of Changes. This uncanny blueprint, now in the hands of the scion of Russian aristocracy, detailed an imminent restructuring of the political and social boundaries of Europe.[3]

But few grasped Germain's true purpose during this time of historic critical mass: not even the king and queen of France could comprehend his tragic forewarnings. The Great White Brotherhood—a fellowship of enlightened luminaries—sent the astute diplomat Saint Germain to orchestrate the development of the United States of Europe. Not only a harbinger of European diplomacy, he made his presence in America during the germinal days of this country. Esoteric scholars say he urged the signing of the Declaration of Independence in a moment of collective fear—a fear of treason and ultimately death. Urging the forefathers to proceed, a shadowed figure in the back of the room shouted: Sign that document!

---

3. K. Paul Johnson, *The Masters Revealed: Madame Blavatsky and the Myth of the Great White Lodge (Suny Series in Western Esoteric Traditions)* (Albany, NY: State University of New York Press), page 19.

To this day, the ironclad identity of this person remains a mystery, though some mystics believe it was Saint Germain. Nevertheless, his avid support spurred the flurry of signatures, sealing the fate of America—and the beginning of Sir Francis Bacon's democratic experiment.

The Comte de Saint Germain never could shape a congealed Europe, but he did form a lasting and profound relationship with America. Germain's present-day participation in U.S. politics reaches the Oval Office. Some theosophical mystics say Germain visits the president of the United States the day after the leader's inauguration; others suggest he's the fabled patriot Uncle Sam.

Saint Germain identifies with the qualities of Brotherhood and freedom. He is the sponsor of humanity and serves as a conduit of Violet Light—a force some claim is powerful enough to propel one into Ascension.

El Morya:

El Morya incarnated from a long line of historical notables, including the fabled King Arthur of England; the Renaissance scholar Sir Thomas Moore, author of Utopia; the patron saint of Ireland, Saint Patrick; and a Rajput prince. El Morya is even linked to the Hebrew patriarch Abraham. But in spite of his illustrious lifetimes, El Morya is best known as Melchior, one of the Magi who followed the Star of Bethlehem to the Christ infant.

El Morya first revealed himself to the founder of the Theosophical Society Helena Petrovna Blavatasky—also known as Madame Blavatsky or H. P. B.—during her childhood in London; that mid-nineteenth century meeting forged a lifelong connection with her Master and other members of the Spiritual Hierarchy. Some esoteric scholars recount different, more dramatic scenarios of their initial introduction. Blavatsky herself claimed El Morya rescued her from a suicide attempt on Waterloo Bridge.[4] The gracious Master dissuaded her from plunging into the waters of the Thames River.

---

4. Papastavro, Tellis S., *The Gnosis and the Law* (Tucson, AZ: Group Avatar), page 53.

Others say the two met in Hyde Park or on a London street. According to Blavatsky, El Morya appeared under a secret political cover as the Sikh prince Maharaja Ranbir Singh of Kashmir, who served as a physically incarnated prototype of Master M. Singh and died in 1885.

Metaphysical scholars credit Blavatsky's work as the impetus for present-day theosophical philosophy and the conception of the Great White Brotherhood. Devoted disciples learned of the Hindu teacher from Blavatsky's childhood visions, and later on in a series of correspondences known as the Mahatma Letters, which contained spiritual guidelines for humanity. El Morya's presence in H. P. B.'s life enriched her spiritual knowledge, and she shared this transformation in a prolific body of texts and writings, namely Isis Unveiled and The Secret Doctrine. During a visit with Madame Blavatsky, A.P. Sinnett, an English newspaper editor, found the first of these letters among the branches of a tree. Over the years, the true meaning and authorship of the Mahatma Letters, reportedly co-authored by fellow Mahatma Kuthumi, have spurned controversy; some say Blavatsky herself forged the messages.

Master M. is associated with the Blue Ray of power, faith, and good will; the Golden City of Gobean; and the planet Mercury. A strict disciplinarian, El Morya dedicates his work to the development of the will. He assists many disciples in discovering personal truths, exploring self-development, and honing the practice of the esoteric discipline. El Morya passes this wisdom to his numerous chelas and students.

The Maha Chohan—El Morya's guru, Lord of the Seven Rays and the Steward of Earth and its evolutions—educated him during his Earthly incarnations in India, Egypt, and Tibet. Declining the Ascension a number of times, it is said that El Morya finally accepted this divine passage in 1888, ascending with his beloved pet dog and horse. (Esoteric symbols of friendship and healing.)

Lord Sananda:

During his paradigm-altering incarnation more than 2,000 years ago, Lord Sananda, also known as Sananda Kumara, embodied the Christ Consciousness, as Jesus, son of God. Some esoteric scholars say he's one of the four sons of Brahma—Sanaka, Sanatana, Sanat-Kumara, and Sanandana— his namesake. According to Vedic lore, the foursome possess eternally liberated souls and live in Tapaloka, the dimension of the great sages. Before manifesting in physical form, Jesus belonged to the Angelic Kingdom. His name was Micah—the Great Angel of Unity. Micah is the son of Archangel Michael who led the Israelites out of Egypt. [5] [For more information on the story of Jesus' life, I recommend reading, *Twelve World Teachers*, by Manly P. Hall.]

Sananda Kumara revealed his identity to the mystic Sister Thedra. Her Master first contacted her in the early 1960s and instructed her to move to Peru, specifically, to a hidden monastery in the Andes mountains. There, undergoing an intense spiritual training, she kept in constant contact with Sananda, and he shared with her prophecies of the coming Earth Changes. After leaving the abbey, Sister Thedra moved to Mt. Shasta, California where she founded the Association of Sananda and Sanat Kumara. She died in 1992.

Sananda posed for a photograph on June 1, 1961 in Chichen Itza, Yucatan. He told Sister Thedra that though the image is valid, he is not limited by form of any kind; therefore, he may take on any appearance necessary. [See *Freedom Star, Prophecies that Heal Earth*].

Serapis Bey:

The lore of Serapis Bey is heavily linked to the story of Helena Blavatsky, Master M., K. H., and the founding of the Theosophical Society. According to lore, Serapis Bey incarnated as Paolos Metamon, an Egyptian magician. Metamon and Blavatsky connected in the mid-1850s during her wanderlust years in the Middle East. H. P. B. soon became his

---

5. Luk, A. D. K., *Law of Life, Book II* (Pueblo, CO: ADK Luk Publications), page 275.

pupil. He introduced her to the secret world of the occult and possibly served as her first physical Master. But many esoteric scholars disagree; they say the Ascended Master of the Fourth Ray is rooted in the Greco-Egyptian mysteries, and appropriately so. Before his Ascension in 400 B.C., Serapis Bey embodied as a high priest at the Ascension Temple of Atlantis more than 11,000 years ago. Other myths put the Master—carrying the Flame of Ascension to Egypt by boat—at the banks of the Nile River near Luxor before the demise of Atlantis and the Earth Changes of Dvapara Yuga.[6] He also incarnated as the Egyptian pharaohs Akhenaton IV and Amenophis III; the heroic King Leonidas of Sparta; and Phidias, the great architect of the Parthenon, the temple of the Goddess Athena, and the colossal statue of Zeus.

A tireless and strict disciplinarian, Serapis Bey, the Master Teacher of Ascension, identifies and prepares souls for Ascension. He accomplishes this by the destruction of the lower self, the state of animal-man, that is captivated by worldly ignorance. And when the corporeal attachments dissolve, the Real Self emerges, a step essential to the attainment of Ascension. The Ancient Egyptians followed a similar practice in their Temples of Serapis. Priests carried out initiatory rites involving rigorous and severe rituals; symbolic illusions of the lower world through which the soul of man wanders for the truth. Those who survived the ordeal were ushered into the presence of Serapis—an awe-inspiring figure, illumined in unseen lights. Serapis became known as the Adversary or the Trier who tested the souls of those seeking union with the Immortals, the Ascension.[7] Serapis Bey serves on the Fourth Ray—it is associated with the absence of color, white; harmony through conflict; and the path of beauty.

The number seven plays a significant role in the worship of this Ascended Master. It begins with his name—Serapis—which contains seven letters. During worship, disciples chant

---

6. Luk, A. D. K., *Law of Life, Book II* (Pueblo, CO: ADK Luk Publications), pages 277-279.

7. Manly Hall, *The Secret Teachings of All Ages*, Diamond Jubilee Edition (Los Angeles: Philosophical Research Society), pages 26-27.

hymns comprising seven vowels, the seven primary sounds. And when expressed in imagery, Serapis wears a crown of seven Rays, symbolizing the seven divine intelligences represented through solar light. Meanwhile, the word "serapis" has many associations: it is the ancient term for Sun; in Hebrew it means "to blaze out"; and it is the soul, enmeshed with the form during physical life, which escapes from the body at death.

Mother Mary, the Western Goddess and Archetype of the Feminine

The Ascended Master and Western Goddess of the Feminine Archetype was an initiate of the ethereal Temples of Nature before her incarnation as Mary, Mother of Jesus Christ. It is claimed that as a child Mary was raised in the mystical traditions of the Essenes, and throughout her lifetime as Mother Mary, she was constantly overshadowed by the Angelic Kingdom. Some Ascended Master texts claim Mary was once a member of the heavenly realm.

Mary's lifetime as the mother of Jesus Christ was planned in-between lifetimes on Earth, "Her embodiment as Mother of Jesus was in the Divine Plan long before she entered the physical realm. She went through a severe initiation at inner levels to test her strength some time before taking embodiment."[5] Throughout her life as the Master's mother, Mary was attuned to the spiritual planes which gave her strength and insight to fulfill her role as the Mother of Jesus. And, no doubt, Mary or Maryam, as she is known in Aramaic, lived in perilous times. The Biblical story in the Book of Matthew accounts the Holy Family's flight to Egypt to avoid King Herod's Massacre of the Innocents. It is claimed that Mother Mary made a vow to assist anyone who had lost their life as a Christian martyr to obtain the Ascension in a future life.[8] Mary the Mother of Jesus became an archetype of the Cosmic Mother for all of humanity.

---

8. A. D. K. Luk, *Points Law of Life, Book II, (ADK Luk Publications, 1989, Pueblo, CO), page 344.*

As an archetype of the Feminine, Mary is also a form of Isis, the Virgin of the World of Hermetic Teaching. The name Isis draws its meaning from Hebrew and Greek sources, which means wisdom or to serve.[9] However, the myth of the Virgin Goddess is contained in the ancient language of Scandinavia as Isa; and is similarly portrayed as the Eleusian Goddess Ceres and Queen Moo of the Mayans. Manly Hall writes, "She was known as the Goddess with ten-thousand appellations and was meta-morphosed by Christianity into the Virgin Mary, for Isis, although she gave birth to all living things— chief among them the Sun—still remained a virgin, according to legendary accounts." As the eldest daughter of Kronus the Ancient Titan, and the wife and sister to Osiris, Isis was the student of the great Master Hermes Trismegistus. Through this affiliation it is claimed the laws for humanity were developed, including an alphabet for written language, astronomy, and the science of seamanship. Isis helped humanity to overcome paternal tyranny through instructing men to love women and children to love and respect their elders through the philosophic teachings of beauty as truth, and the intrinsic value of justice. The teachings of Isis are not for the irreverent. The discipline of emotion and the acquisition of wisdom are required in order to access and understand the evolutionary energies of the Feminine. Ancient initiates were advised to keep silent their venerated knowledge of the spiritual truths underlying the vulgar and profane.[10]

In Christianity Mary is known as the Virgin Mother of Jesus; however, Catholics and Protestants differ regarding their worship of the Mother of the Son of God. In Islam, the Virgin Mary is esteemed as the mother to the Prophet Issa.[11] Jesus' birth was prophesied by the Archangel Gabriel in a

---

9. Manly P. Hall, *The Secret Teachings of All Ages: An Encyclopedic Outline of Masonic, Hermetic, Qabbalistic and Rosicrucian Symbolical Philosophy*, (Philosophical Research Society, Inc., 1988, Los Angeles, CA), page 45.

10. *Ibid.*, page 44.

11. Wikipedia, *Mary (Mother of Jesus)*, http://en.wikipedia.org/wiki/Mary_(mother_of_jesus), (2009).

visit to Mary during her betrothal to Joseph, and the Archangel declared, "She was to be the mother of the promised Messiah by conceiving him through the Holy Spirit."[12] The New Testament places Mary at Nazareth in Galilee, the daughter of Joachim and Anne. Apocryphal legend claims Mary's birth was also a miracle—her mother was barren. To many Roman Catholics, Mary was the perfect vessel to carry the Christ, and was "filled with grace from the very moment of her conception in her mother's womb and the stain of original sin."[13] This spiritual precept is known as the Immaculate Conception of Mary.

Contemporary interpretations of the Immaculate Concept state this spiritual practice is the Alchemy of holding the image of perfection through the use of prayer, meditation, and visualization. Thought-forms of "Beauty, poise, and grace on behalf of others," is claimed to create Divine Energies of purity and protection.[14] David C. Lewis writes regarding the spiritual exercise of holding the Immaculate Concept for ourselves:

"Ultimately we must first hold the immaculate concept for ourselves by attuning to our own Higher Self and maintaining a vigil of Oneness through presence and awareness of our own Divine Nature. Once we have learned to live in this unified field of stillness and beingness and maintain our spiritual poise, especially during challenging times and situations, we can more easily practice the science of the immaculate concept on behalf of others."[15]

According to the Ascended Masters Mother Mary holds the Immaculate Concept for the incoming generations of the Seventh Manu through the energies of the Swaddling Cloth, located in Brazil, South America. In the I AM America teachings, Mother Mary often merges her energies with Kuan Yin,

12. Wikipedia, Mary (Mother of Jesus), http://en.wikipedia.org/wiki/Mary_(mother_of_jesus), (2009).
13. Ibid.
14. David C. Lewis, "The Immaculate Concept: Creating Alchemical Change," http://www.theheartscenter.org, (2009).
15. Ibid.

the Feminine Bodhisattva of Mercy and Compassion, and together they channel the energies of the Divine Mother to Earth. Divine Mother is an archetype of Feminine Unity and the ONE. Beloved Mary is known to appear at times of physical or emotional crisis, often to convey the healing power of wholeness and unconditional love. Mother Mary's Temple of the Sacred Heart, located in the Fifth Dimension, prepares souls for re-embodiment.[16] She is the Ascended Master sponsor of the Golden City of Marnero, located in Mexico. Marnero means the ocean of candles; its quality is Virtue; and this Golden City is affiliated with the Green Ray.

Soltec, Ascended Master of the Celestial Brotherhood

Beloved Soltec is an Ascended Master from a different solar system, and perhaps a different galaxy altogether. He is the ultimate brainiac, and is focused on the use of the sciences and human technology for the upliftment and ascension of humanity. He originally came to Earth through the mission of the well-known Ashtar Command, a group of Ascended Masters and Galactic Beings who are pledged to shepherd humanity's spiritual development at specific critical junctures. Through this guiding protection, Soltec was the director of numerous missions and scientific patrols to Earth for research and spiritual intervention. He once commented about his spiritual service, "My surveillance responsibilities have been unlike Ashtar's in that my mission is the gathering of facts and scientific data that can in turn be used for the betterment of Humanity and this Solar System. The mission of Ashtar has been the spiritual education of a backward planet and the ascension of its inhabitants through initiations and gathering of information designed for that purpose."[17] He applies compassion and love with logical precision, and transmits the Will of God with the skill of a seasoned Archangel. The Ashtar Command often works side-by-side with Earth's Angelic Host through the Celestial Brotherhood, although

16. A. D. K Luk, *Points Law of Life, Book II*, (ADK Luk Publications, 1989, Pueblo, CO), page 347.
17. *Ashtar, a Tribute* Compiles by Tuella. Accessed March 13, 2019. https://www. thenewearth.org/AshtarTribute.html.

they are not considered part of this divine kingdom. Soltec is the hierarch of Pashacino, the sixth Golden City located in Alberta and British Columbia, Canada. This sublime Golden City of the Green Ray serves as a Bridge of Brotherhood for all people.

Discography

This list provides the recording session date and name of the original selected recordings cited in this work that provide the basis for its original transcriptions.

Toye, Lori

Twilight Meditation originally *Luminous Light One*, I AM America Seventh Ray Publishing International, MP3, ℗ © January 29, 2010.

Luminous Light originally *Luminous Light Two*, I AM America Seventh Ray Publishing International, MP3, ℗ © February 18, 2010.

HU-man Wave, I AM America Seventh Ray Publishing International, MP3, ℗ © February 25, 2010.

Evolutionary Body, I AM America Seventh Ray Publishing International, MP3, ℗ © March 19, 2010.

Evolution Equals Revolution, I AM America Seventh Ray Publishing International, MP3, ℗ © March 25, 2010.

Index

About Lori and Lenard Toye

Lori Toye is not a Prophet of doom and gloom. The fact that she became a Prophet at all is highly unlikely. Reared in a small Idaho farming community as a member of the conservative Missouri Synod Lutheran church, Lori had never heard of meditation, spiritual development, reincarnation, channeling, or clairvoyant sight.

Her unusual spiritual journey began in Washington State, when, as advertising manager of a weekly newspaper, she answered a request to pick up an ad for a local health food store. As she entered, a woman at the counter pointed a finger at her and said, "You have work to do for Master Saint Germain!"

The next several years were filled with spiritual enlightenment that introduced Lori, then only twenty-two years old, to the most exceptional and inspirational information she had ever encountered. Lori became a student of Ascended Master teachings.

Awakened one night by the luminous figure of Saint Germain at the foot of her bed, her work had begun. Later in the same year, an image of a map appeared in her dream. Four teachers clad in white robes were present, pointing out Earth Changes that would shape the future United States.

Five years later, faced with the stress of a painful divorce and rebuilding her life as a single mother, Lori attended spiritual meditation classes. While there, she shared her experience, and encouraged by friends, she began to explore the dream through daily meditation. The four Beings appeared again, and expressed a willingness to share the information. Over a six-month period, they gave over eighty sessions of material, including detailed information that would later become the I AM America Map.

Clearly she had to produce the map. The only means to finance it was to sell her house. She put her home up for sale, and in a depressed market, it sold the first day at full asking price.

She produced the map in 1989, rolled copies of them on her kitchen table, and sold them through word-of-mouth. She then launched a lecture tour of the Northwest and California. Hers was the first Earth Changes Map published, and many others have followed, but the rest is history.

From the tabloids to the *New York Times*, *The Washington Post*, television interviews in the U.S., London, and Europe, Lori's Mission was to honor the material she had received. The material is not hers, she stresses. It belongs to the Masters, and their loving, healing approach is disseminated through the I AM America Publishing Company operated by her husband and spiritual partner, Lenard Toye.

Lenard Toye, originally from Philadelphia, PA, was born into a family of professional contractors and builders, and has a remarkable singing voice. Lenard's compelling tenor voice replaced many of the greats at a moment's notice—Pavarotti and Domingo, including many performances throughout Europe. When he retired from music, he joined his family's business yet pursued his personal interests in alternative healing.

He attended *Barbara Brennan's School of Healing* to further develop the gift of auric vision. Working together with his wife Lori, they organized free classes of healing techniques and the channeled teachings. Their instructional pursuits led them to form the *School of the Four Pillars* which includes holistic and energy healing and Ascended Master Teachings. In 1995 and 1996 they sponsored the first Prophecy Conferences in Philadelphia and Phoenix, Arizona. His management and sales background has played a very important role in his partnership with his wife Lori and their publishing company. Other publications include three additional Prophecy maps, thirteen books, a video, and more than sixty audio tapes based on sessions with Master Teacher Saint Germain and other Ascended Masters.

Spiritual in nature, I AM America is not a church, religion, sect, or cult. There is no interest or intent in amassing followers or engaging in any activity other than what Lori and Lenard can do on their own to publicize the materials they have been entrusted with.

They have also been directed to build the first Golden City community. A very positive aspect of the vision is that all the maps include areas called, "Golden Cities." These places hold a high spiritual energy, and are where sustainable communities are to be built using solar energy alongside classical feng shui engineering and infrastructure. The first community, Wenima Village, is currently being planned for development.

Concerned that some might misinterpret the Maps' messages as doom and gloom and miss the metaphor for personal change, or not consider the spiritual teachings attached to the maps, Lori emphasizes that the Masters stressed that this was a Prophecy of choice. Prophecy allows for choice in making informed decisions and promotes the opportunity for cooperation and harmony. Lenard and Lori's vision for I AM America is to share the Ascended Masters' prophecies as spiritual warnings to heal and renew our lives.

Books by Lori Toye

Books:

NEW WORLD WISDOM SERIES: *Book One, Two, and Three*

FREEDOM STAR: *Prophecies that Heal Earth*

THE EVER PRESENT NOW: *A New Understanding of Consciousness and Prophecy*

I AM AMERICA ATLAS: *Based on the Maps, Prophecies, and Teachings of the Ascended Masters*

GOLDEN CITIES AND THE MASTERS OF SHAMBALLA: *The I AM America Teachings*

GOLDEN CITY SERIES
  Book One: Points of Perception
  Book Two: Light of Awakening
  Book Three: Divine Destiny
  Book Four: Sacred Energies of the Golden Cities
  Book Five: Temples of Consciousness
  Book Six: Awaken the Master Within
  Book Seven: Soul Alchemy (Advanced students only)

I AM AMERICA TRILOGY
  Book One: A Teacher Appears
  Book Two: Sisters of the Flame
  Book Three: Fields of Light

I AM AMERICA COLLECTION
  Sacred Fire: A Handbook for Spiritual Growth and
    Personal Development
  Building the Seamless Garment

Maps by Lori Toye

Maps:
I AM America Map
Freedom Star World Map
United States 6-Map Scenario
United States Golden City Map

A M E R I C A

I AM AMERICA PUBLISHING & DISTRIBUTING
P.O. Box 2511, Payson, Arizona, 85547, USA. (928) 978-6435

For More Information:
www.iamamerica.com
www.loritoye.com

About I AM America

I AM America is an educational and publishing foundation
dedicated to disseminating the Ascended Masters' message
of Earth Changes Prophecy and Spiritual Teachings for self-
development. Our office is run by the husband and wife team
of Lenard and Lori Toye who hand-roll maps, package, and mail
information and products with a small staff. Our first publication
was the I AM America Map, which was published in September
1989. Since then we have published three more Prophecy maps,
thirteen books, and numerous recordings based on the channeled
sessions with the Spiritual Teachers.

We are not a church, a religion, a sect, or cult and are not
interested in amassing followers or members. Nor do we have any
affiliation with a church, religion, political group, or government
of any kind. We are not a college or university, research facility,
or a mystery school. El Morya told us that the best way to see
ourselves is as, "Cosmic Beings, having a human experience."

In 1994, we asked Saint Germain, "How do you see our
work at I AM America?" and he answered, "I AM America
is to be a clearinghouse for the new humanity." Grabbing a
dictionary, we quickly learned that the term "clearinghouse"
refers to "an organization or unit within an organization
that functions as a central agency for collecting, organizing,
storing, and disseminating documents, usually within a specific
academic discipline or field." So inarguably, we are this too.
But in uncomplicated terms, we publish and share spiritually
transformational information because at I AM America there is no
doubt that, "A Change of Heart can Change the World."

With Violet Flame Blessings,
Lori & Lenard Toye

For more information or to visit our online bookstore, go to:
www.iamamerica.com
www.loritoye.com
I AM America / P.O. Box 2511
Payson, AZ 85547

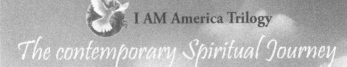

I AM America Trilogy

The contemporary Spiritual Journey

A Teacher Appears	Sisters of the Flame	Fields of Light
ISBN: 978180050446	ISBN: 978180050262	ISBN: 978180050613
254 pages	216 pages	310 pages

This series of insightful books, written by the creator of the acclaimed *I AM America Maps* shares a fresh and personal viewpoint of the contemporary spiritual journey. Lori Toye was just twenty-two years old when she first encountered Ascended Master teaching. The *I AM America Trilogy* takes us back to the beginning of her experiences with her spiritual teachers and includes insights that have never been disclosed in any previous books or writings. In "A Teacher Appears," learn how true wisdom and the inner teacher is within all of us. "Sisters of the Flame," continues an initiatory passage into the feminine with the Cellular Awakening. "Fields of Light," explains how to integrate and Master our spiritual light through soul-transcending teachings of Ascension. Lori's personal story is interwoven throughout the I AM America Trilogy in a rich tapestry of spiritual techniques, universal wisdom, and knowledge gained through a life-changing spiritual journey.

I AM America Atlas

Updated Edition!
Contains all of the
I AM America Maps
Full color
Over 100 Maps
164 pages

New World Wisdom Series

Spiritual Teachings from
the Ascended Masters
Books One, Two, and Three

Spiritual Teaching for the New Times

For more information:
loritoye.com
iamamerica.com
or call (928) 978-6435

Navigating the
New Earth

I AM America Map
US Earth Changes
Order #001

Freedom Star Map
World Earth Changes
Order #004

Since 1989, I AM America has been publishing
thought-provoking information on Earth Changes.
All of our Maps feature the compelling cartography of
the New Times illustrated with careful details and
unique graphics. Professionally presented in full color.
Explore the prophetic possibilities!

Retail and Wholesale prices available.

Purchase Maps at:

www.IAMAMERICA.com

**6-Map
Scenario**
US Earth
Changes
Progression
Order #022

**Golden Cities
Map**
United States
Order #110

AMERICA

P.O. Box 2511
Payson, Arizona
(480) 744-6188

CPSIA information can be obtained
at www.ICGtesting.com
Printed in the USA
BVHW082137030720
582863BV00001B/67